A2 12SC

HIDDEN TREASURES
OF SANTA CRUZ COUNTY

Betty Bane

HIDDEN TREASURES
OF SANTA CRUZ COUNTY

Betty Barr

BrockingJ Books   Sonoita, Arizona

To contact the author or order
additional copies of this book
write to us at:
P.O. Box 226
Sonoita, Arizona 85637

This edition was prepared for printing by
Ghost River Images
5350 East Fourth Street
Tucson, Arizona 85711
ghostriverimages.com

On the cover: Adobe barn with traditional tin roof was built in the early 1900s at Patti and Andy Kelly's Umpire Ranch in Canelo.
Betty Barr photo

Back cover photo of the author by John Barr

Library of Congress Control Number: 2006907581

Printed in the United States of America

First Printing: September, 2006

10 9 8 7 6 5 4 3 2 1

Contents

Dedicated to Bob Bowman

Historian, mentor and friend

Acknowledgments

I owe a tremendous debt of gratitude to the true "Hidden Treasures," the many families who opened their homes and hearts to me and shared stories of their pioneering ancestors who settled the eastern part of Santa Cruz County. As I sat across so many kitchen tables over the past ten years, sharing coffee and comfort food, I realized that country hospitality is as welcoming today as it was when the early settlers first forged a life in this area. Their stories, passed down by word of mouth from parents to children and grandchildren, brought smiles, a few real belly laughs and an occasional tear, as descendants of these hardy settlers recounted the joys and hardships faced by those whose courage and spirit played an integral role in the formation of the county.

A special thanks to Howard Hathaway, now deceased, who shared his memoirs and photographs of his father, Jim Hathaway, and to Howard's sister, Marion Bittinger, and son, Dick, who generously provided additional pictures and allowed me to base some stories on Howard's copyrighted materials. Thank you also to Jim Hathaway's grandchildren Jim McClellan and Sandy Kuntz. I am also indebted to Susan Ingram Hughes, of the Empire Ranch Foundation, for her expertise and assistance with many aspects of the Empire Ranch history, stories of her mother, Dusty Vail, and archival photographs of the Vail era.

Mere thanks cannot express my gratitude to Bob Bowman who has been by my side every step of the way and without whom this book would never have gotten off the ground. Joe and Noemi Quiroga filled me in on the intricacies of the Hispanic cultural influences in the county, and Joe was my enthusiastic guide and patient interpreter at the beargrass cutters' camp. Two sisters, Jane Woods and Marka Moss, not only provided invaluable information on pioneers on both sides of their family, but also guided me on a historic journey through Black Oak Pioneer Cemetery, complete with reminiscences on many of the families buried there.

Thank you to physician and poet, Dr. Paul Duffey of Tucson, who shared memories of picnics and Easter sunrise services at Sunnyside and allowed me to include two of his poems in this collection. Harold Hagar scanned many photos for me. Author Sinclair Browning graciously agreed to write the introduction and provided technical assistance and unbounded encouragement when the going got rough.

A big thank you to Bob Kimball, former editor and publisher of the Nogales International and the Bulletin, for his faith in me when I submitted my first historic feature back in 1998. His confidence in my work and his continued support of my efforts has meant a lot.

I was truly fortunate to have three excellent proofreaders who made a supreme effort to catch my many errors. Their individual areas of expertise complimented each other perfectly. Susan L. Miller's incisive editorial comments were invaluable, Nadene Hicks cleared up much of my "comma confusion," and Sylvia Hamel's knowledge of the county and the ranching industry was a tremendous asset.

Many of the stories on the following pages have appeared previously in the Nogales International/Bulletin newspapers, a division of Wick Communications Company. My heartfelt thanks to the company and to Manuel Coppola, editor and publisher, for their interest in publishing historical features in the local press.

Finally, thank you to my family, especially my cousin, Tom Newmeyer, who has been my biggest fan; my sister Patti Kelly, proof reader, map designer and all-around cheerleader; and my husband, John, without whose support I would never have persevered.

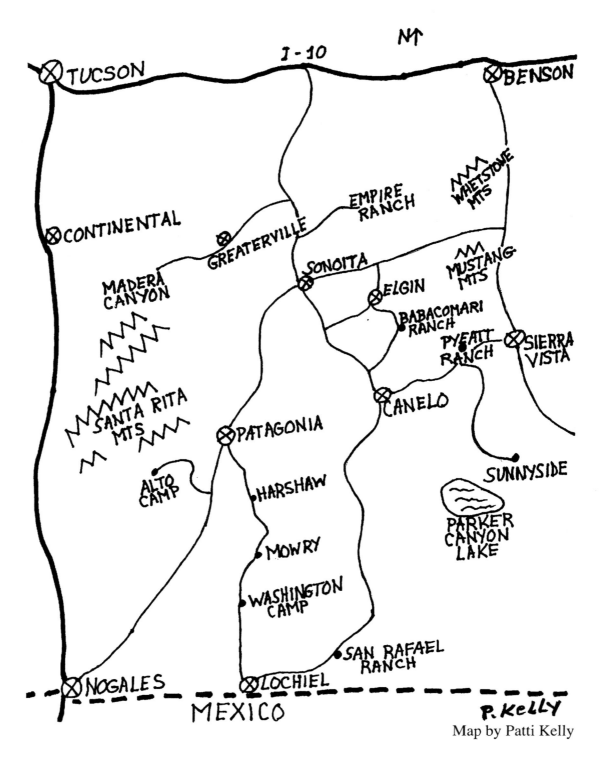

N↑

I-10

TUCSON
BENSON
CONTINENTAL
GREATERVILLE
EMPIRE RANCH
WHETSTONE MTS
MADERA CANYON
SONOITA
MUSTANG MTS
ELGIN
BABACOMARI RANCH
PYEATT RANCH
SIERRA VISTA
SANTA RITA MTS
CANELO
PATAGONIA
SUNNYSIDE
ALTO CAMP
HARSHAW
PARKER CANYON LAKE
MOWRY
WASHINGTON CAMP
SAN RAFAEL RANCH
NOGALES
LOCHIEL
MEXICO

P. Kelly
Map by Patti Kelly

10

Introduction

Hidden Treasures could not be more aptly named. Author Betty Barr has indeed mined some wonderful stories that would have otherwise been lost.

Those of us fortunate enough to live in Southeastern Arizona know what a special place this is. While we're still lucky enough to have working ranches in this corner of our state, it's clear that ranching and the cowboy way of life are quickly disappearing.

As we ride and hike this incredible country we often find remnants of those who came before. A crumbling adobe wall, a dam made of rock that rivals the finest mosaic murals, collapsed loading chutes and splintered wooden corrals, a caved-in mine shaft, an abandoned railroad bridge...all have stories behind them. Most of them, unfortunately, have died with the people who lived them.

But thanks to Betty's keen curiosity and hard labor some of the histories of the early Santa Cruz settlers have been captured so we can all enjoy them. Her painstaking research, coupled with interviews of the people who settled this county, and their descendants, have produced the treasure that is now in your hands. Because of that effort, while the wooden corrals dissolve to dust and the adobe returns to the earth, these stories will live on.

As well they should.

I am pleased to introduce this book because it honors the hard work, determination and grit of those pioneers who first settled this extraordinary land.

I am grateful to them.

And to you, Betty, for recording these valuable pieces of history.

Thank you.

Sinclair Browning

Magnificent memorial, commemorating the passage of Fray Marcos de Niza through the San Rafael Valley in 1539, is located a few steps from the U.S./Mexico border at Lochiel. According to legend, de Niza was searching for the Seven Cities of Cibola, purportedly paved in gold, and was the first white man to venture this far north.
Barr photo.

Foreword

Arizona's eastern Santa Cruz County, a lush corridor of rolling grasslands, natural springs and heavily wooded mountains, extends southward from the Pima County line to the Mexican border. Panoramic mountain vistas stretch from the majestic Santa Rita Mountains at its western edge to the Huachuca and Whetstones in the east. The secrets hidden within this unique landscape weave a rich historical tapestry of multicultural diversity. From the earliest Indian inhabitants to the Spanish explorers and missionaries, gold-crazed miners, adventurous military men, Mexican and Chinese laborers and finally, the westward-moving pioneers and homesteaders, each one of them contributed, in his own unique way, to the formation of the county as we know it today.

Spanish explorer, Fray Marcos de Niza, accompanied by the Moorish slave, Estavanico, came north from Mexico in 1539 searching for the Seven Cities of Cibola. De Niza was purportedly the first European to enter Arizona, when the pair came through the San Rafael Valley near Lochiel. When Estavanico was killed by Indians in a pueblo in New Mexico, the frightened de Niza fled back to Mexico without locating his quest.

The following year, 1540, Francisco Vasquez Coronado, lured by de Niza's extravagant and fictitious claims of seeing the riches of Cibola, traveled across Arizona as far as Kansas in a vain search for the city. His adherence to the Spanish policy of Indian murder and enslavement is generally credited with sowing the original seeds of hatred for the European in the southwestern Indian tribes.

Almost a century later, in 1691, Father Eusebio Francisco Kino, a Jesuit missionary and explorer, traveled north from Mexico, coming into Arizona through the San Rafael Valley. He continued over the Canelo Pass to the Babacomari River, where he encountered the peaceful Pima Indian farming tribe known as the Huachucas. Their cultivated fields lay along the creek near the present town of Elgin. Kino located another Indian village, Los Reyes de Sonoidag, at the head of

13

Sonoita Creek, in the Fort Crittendon area. Sonoita is a Papago Indian (now Tohono O'odham) term, meaning "where the corn grows green." No Indian ever raised a hand against Father Kino, who traveled extensively throughout Mexico and Arizona establishing numerous missions before his death and burial in Magdelana, Mexico, in 17ll. A statue of Father Kino, representing the State of Arizona, was unveiled at the Capitol Rotunda in Washington, D.C., February 15, 1965.

Father Kino introduced cattle into the Santa Cruz Valley and established several ranches. In an attempt to encourage settlement in the area, Spain granted land to settlers living inside the presidio boundaries. Warring Apaches drove many of the settlers away, but when Mexico gained independence from Spain in 1821, more large land grants were created. The Baca Float Ranch combined the old Tumacacori, Calabasas and Guevavi grants into a ranch of 100,000 acres. Other early land grants included the San Rafael de la Zanja, San Jose de Sonoita, Babacomari and Canoa. Many of the grants remained abandoned after the Civil War and squatters moved in, built houses and operated cattle ranches, although they did not hold official title to the land. Eventually, the Mexican grants were sold to Americans and the squatters were forced to move.

Fort Buchanan (later Fort Crittenden) was established in 1856 to help control the Indians, protect settlers and create a mail route across southern United States. The fort consisted of a cluster of stables and huts along the Sonoita Creek, about one mile west of present-day Sonoita. Post Commander, Captain Richard Ewell, led bloody skirmishes against the Apaches culminating with the infamous "Bascom Affair." George Bascom, a new second lieutenant from West Point, bungled the handling of a hostage situation with the formerly-friendly Apache chief, Cochise, which led the tribe to turn against the Americans. With the outbreak of the Civil War in 1861, Arizona's troops were sent to the front and Fort Buchanan was abandoned. The Apaches, no longer fearing punishment, raided at will for the next 30 years, driving many miners, ranchers and farmers from the area. The Apache wars finally ended with the capture of Geronimo in 1886.

President Abraham Lincoln signed the Homestead Act into law May, 1862, to encourage westward migration after the Civil War. For a $10 filing fee, any citizen, man, woman, slave or freeman, could claim 160 acres. To "prove up" on the claim, the applicant had to be 21 years of age and was granted five years to live, build a dwelling on the land, make improvements and plant at least 40 acres with some kind of crop. Many families flocked to eastern Santa Cruz County to take advantage of this "free land," and cultivated fields of beans, corn, hegira or milo maize. The "dry farming" method used no irrigation; crops lived or died depending on the amount of rainfall each season. During periods of drought, many gave up and moved away, relinquishing their homesteads. Those who had money were able to buy up these "relinquishments," for a nominal sum, adding to their holdings. Eventually, most realized that dry farming was not a viable endeavor, and turned to cattle ranching to make a living.

In June of 1881 the Santa Fe Railroad proposed extending their tracks 88 miles to meet up with the Mexican train coming up from Sonora to Nogales. Construction

A picnic at the Hummel Ranch near Sonoita was held to plan a Fairgrounds for Santa Cruz County. The Fairgrounds, near Sonoita, was incorporated in 1915 and has become the heart of community activities in the county. Circa 1910.
Photo courtesy Bowman Archives Room.

began at Fairbanks on the San Pedro River and proceeded west across the Babacomari Ranch, through Sonoita and Patagonia, southward to Nogales. The railroad was a boon to the farming, mining and ranching communities and also boasted passenger service. There were two trains a day, one for freight and one for passengers.

By the early 1900s, the county was dotted with one-room schools, mining and ranching enterprises were flourishing and families rode miles over rough terrain on horseback, buggies or wagons to meet up with their far-flung neighbors for picnics, dances and church services. On September 12, 1914, a group of local families gathered at the Hummel Ranch for a picnic and meeting to discuss forming an association so that they could put on an annual fair. This was the beginning of the Santa Cruz County Fair and Rodeo Association, which operates the fairgrounds at Sonoita, and remains the center of community activities to this day.

Captured on the following pages are the memories of those by-gone days, recounted by the people who lived them and their descendants. There are a legion of other stories still hidden in hills and valleys, waiting to be told another day.

Patagonia Depot, built around 1914, is a landmark in the town. A rare snowstorm in 1985 blanketed the trees.
Paul Mahalik photo, courtesy Bowman Archives Room.

Dr. Delmar Mock

Patagonia

Dr. Mock greets visitors with a bone-crushing handshake that belies his 90 years and a mischievous twinkle of the eye that evokes memories of his legendary humor. He attributes his superman grip to a boyhood spent milking cows on his father's farm in western Kansas -the humor seems to be a lifelong trait. This old-time country doctor grew up a sickly youth of small physical stature and flaming red hair whose pranks and loving nature endeared him to family and schoolmates alike.

Laughter is the best medicine and Dr. Mock practices it with great flair. On one occasion, Bob Bowman's mother fell ill during a visit to his ranch on the Greaterville Road. When Dr. Mock arrived he found her lying on the couch in the living room. Doc sat down on a stool beside the sofa and noticed the elderly woman was holding her hand over her mouth. She said, "I'm sorry Dr. Mock, I don't have my teeth in." Mock said, "Winifred, don't worry about it," and with that he pulled off his flaming red toupee and threw it on the floor.

That wasn't the only time his rug hit the ground - he would often pull off his hair to distract youngsters when he was preparing to give them a shot. Adults, too, often cringed at the thought of an injection. When Posy Piper's mother went in for treatment, she watched as Dr. Mock set out bottles of fluid, added a little from each to the syringe, held it up to the light and added a little more. She decided the cure might be worse than her ailment and claimed that what the locals referred to as a

"Dr. Mock cocktail" made her head spin around and her spit dry up. She had to admit, however, that she began to feel better shortly afterwards.

Delmar Mock graduated from the College of Medical Evangelists (now Loma Linda University) imbued with a zeal to carry out the motto of his alma mater, "To Make Man Whole." He has spent his entire life doing just that. A diagnosis of an allergy to the latex in rubber in his final year dashed his dreams of becoming a surgeon - he was not able to don the gloves required in the operating room. Undaunted, he switched to anesthesiology, "where I watch the other guy do it," and together with Cleo, his loving wife of over 50 years, he has spent a lifetime of dedicated service as a general practitioner and anesthesiologist in the Patagonia area.

He held office hours in Patagonia in the mornings, in Sierra Vista in the afternoons, covered Canelo, Elgin and Patagonia in the evenings, and somehow made time to serve as the anesthesiologist at the hospital in Nogales. His schedule was so tight that many patients remember meeting the "doctor on the run" at the Sonoita Crossroads to get a shot or have their throat swabbed.

Dr. Mock is a devout Seventh-day Adventist and quick to credit the "Great Physician" for cures that have no reasonable explanation. Adventists observe Saturday as the Sabbath and this was cause for concern to some of the locals when the new young doctor first came to town. Early in 1946 a vocal town councilman, Buck Blabon, confronted him on the main street and demanded to know, "What are we supposed to do if one of us gets sick on Saturday?" Mock responded, "Rest assured if someone gets sick on Saturday he will receive prompt treatment. But, if someone gets sick on Monday and waits till Saturday to tell me about it, that might be another story." Blabon never did call the doctor on Saturday and in fact became one of his best friends and loyal patients. He worked for people's spiritual welfare in many ways, welcoming invitations to speak at the community's Easter sunrise services, purchasing Bible slides to be used for evangelism in foreign countries and conducting funerals. He formed such a close friendship with Father Chestnut of the local Catholic parish that the priest contributed $10 a month to the Seventh-Day Adventist Church's mission program and painted a beautiful picture that has long been the focal point of the Mock living room.

The dedicated doctor wore out ten Pontiacs traveling over 2,500 square miles treating patients, and on many occasions, animals as well. He was the only doctor for miles and the closest veterinarian was in Douglas. He pulled porcupine quills from dogs' mouths, milked cows and on one occasion even splinted a canary's leg between two tiny sticks of wood.

He was probably the only doctor in the state equipped with an official law enforcement red light, which he laughingly referred to as the gumball machine. He says he was an "Ornery (not Honorary) Deputy." His patients used signals to alert him to their condition as he drove by their outlying homes, especially in the early years when there was no phone service. A towel tied on the fencepost meant the patient was well; a light left burning on the porch meant his help was needed. When phones were installed his number was Patagonia 10.

His territory extended from the tops of mountain peaks to the depths of mine shafts and all the rolling grasslands in between and his shift was 24 hours a day, seven days a week in all kinds of weather. When a disheveled and distraught hunter appeared at his door at sundown on a chilly November day and announced that his buddy was shot "up on the mountain," Doc, along with Ray Bergier and Henry Acevedo, headed out on horseback. The hunter had been accidentally shot in the stomach and was in critical condition when Doc arrived. After treating the injuries, Doc laid down beside the patient to keep him warm during the night. To supplement the IV during the harrowing stretcher trip down the mountain, Doc plunged a hypodermic needle into his own arm (he is a universal donor) and injected the withdrawn blood into the injured man's arm.

Doc dreaded mining accidents the most. A dynamite charge went off prematurely at Flux Mine and threw two miners about 200 feet down the shaft. Doc and Mr. Rothrock, the coroner, had the duty of going deep into the shaft with the mining officials. They found that the two men had struck the tops and sides of the tunnel as the blast had propelled them on their deadly journey. One of the miners was a family friend, Paul Acevedo, and although Doc dreaded being the bearer of the bad news, part of his ministry was to offer support and consolation to bereaved families in the community. "One cannot attend to this type of occurrence without coming to realize the fragility of life and how we live in a dangerous world," Doc said.

Doc delivered his first baby, a boy born to the Grauer family, on December 16, 1946. His fee was $7. Thirty-seven years later he delivered number 1,500, or maybe it was 2,000 or 2,500, he says. With those kinds of numbers, who's counting. Sleep deprivation was a way of life and Doc learned to take catnaps whenever and wherever he could. If a patient was slow in delivering a baby, Doc was often known to lie down beside her on the bed with the instruction, "Wake me when the baby starts coming."

Some were born in their own homes or the clinic or hospital, but wherever they decided to enter the world, Doc always seemed to make it in time. Posy and Bill Piper called Doc and asked him to meet them at the hospital in Nogales as their

The Delmar R. Mock City Park at the south end of Patagonia was dedicated in honor of Dr. Mock February 27, 1983 and includes play and exercise equipment to encourage the local residents to maintain good health practices.
Barr photo

baby was on its way. Posy thought they were really rushing but when they got to Nogales, Doc was sitting on the hospital porch reading the paper.

"He drove like a bat out of hell," Pete Bidegain says. When Pete had a ruptured pancreas Doc made it from Patagonia to the Babacomari Ranch, a distance of about 25 miles, in 18 minutes flat. He loaded Pete in the back of the Pontiac and with Pete's wife holding the IV elevated out the window they rushed to the emergency

room in Tucson. After surgery the Tucson doctor came to the waiting room to meet the doctor who saved Pete's life, but by that time Doc was halfway back to Patagonia.

Medical careers run in Mock's family. There were 13 doctors and 28 nurses in the clan and Dr. Mock is proud of the fact that all three of his daughters became nurses and his granddaughter went on a six-month medical mission to Africa. Delmar and Cleo Mock celebrated their 50th wedding anniversary August 22, 1990 by repeating their vows at the Patagonia Community Church where they were married. They held hands and sang "Let me call you sweetheart." Afterwards, they rode all over town sitting in the rumble seat of John Ashcraft's Model A, with tin cans tied on the back. All four of their children, Carolyn, Winona, Delma and Delbert, plus many grandchildren, old friends and patients crowded into Thurber Hall for a reception following the ceremonies.

When Dr. Mock appeared in front of the draft board during the Korean War, the Chairman of the Board recommended, "Leave the guy in Patagonia. Only a fool would stay there." To the everlasting gratitude of his many patients and associates, Dr. Mock found his reward in a life of service and dedication in the fool's countryside of Patagonia.

The Bond family (Front row) Joe, Hope and Albert. (Back row) Minnie Ammerman Bond and Josiah Bond. Circa 1914.
Photo courtesy Catherine Bond Elefson.

Josiah and Minnie Bond

Alto Camp

Minnie Ammerman, a beautiful, willowy blonde, was born in Sommerville, New Jersey, in the late 1800s. One evening in 1904 she was outside her family home cutting wood when a young man came by and offered to help her. "My father was working for a mine there," says their youngest daughter, Catherine Bond Elefson. "He went in her yard and said, 'I'll do that for you.' When my son heard the story, years later, he joked that it was no wonder she fell for him."

Josiah Bond was born in Kenosha, Wisconsin, graduated from the Colorado School of Mines and had done some work in Mexico as a mining engineer. While in the West he discovered good mining claims in Alto, a small camp in the Santa Rita Mountains near Patagonia. After he and Minnie were married, he brought her out to Alto and built their adobe home there in 1906.

One of the rooms in the home doubled as the official post office and Minnie Bond was named the first postmistress, June 6, 1912. Catherine remembers ruefully that the United States Government paid no rent for the use of this room.

The young couple was blessed with a growing family: Josiah III (Joe), Albert, Hope, and lastly, Catherine. One daughter, Dorothy, died as an infant and is buried in the family plot on the hillside to the east of the house.

In 1907, when they had only lived in their new house about a year, little Joe wandered away at dusk. When he came to a big cactus on the rim of what was later named Bond Canyon, he lay down and went to sleep. Fearing he had fallen into a mineshaft, the neighbors gathered with carbide lights, candles and kerosene lamps, and fanned out for the search. "Joe had a fabulous memory and while he didn't remember his trip to the cactus, he did remember waking and seeing lights and wondering what it was all about," Catherine remembers. "He was found sleeping under a 'Candle of the Lord' cactus." (People often referred to the ocotillo as the candle of the Lord because of its red blooming tips, reminiscent of candle flames).

One day in the fall of 1922, just a few months after Catherine was born, Minnie set out on horseback with her baby and her 14-year-old son, Albert, to visit neighbors down the canyon. Menacing clouds cut their visit short. According to Albert's future wife, Mary Ann, Minnie wrapped the baby tightly in a slicker and blanket and put her on the front of the saddle. Then she and Albert hurriedly mounted up and turned their horses for home.

To the young boy's horror, a bolt of lightning struck his mother and her horse, killing them both instantly. The seven-month old baby was flung free by the tremendous force of the strike and landed on the hillside. Miraculously, little Catherine's life was spared, her fall possibly cushioned by the blankets her mother had carefully wrapped around her.

Terrified, young Albert galloped home to get his father, crying out that his mother was hurt. In the ensuing chaos, thinking that his beautiful wife had been shot by bandits, Josiah grabbed up a rifle and headed for the scene. Albert finally stammered out that it was a lightning strike and when the two reached the spot, they found Minnie lying dead and the baby safely nearby. Albert was so traumatized by the tragedy, he was not able to speak for months. When he finally spoke again, in the midst of another storm, his first words were, "Where's the baby?"

The Figueroa family and their eleven children lived in their three houses at Alto Camp. The father, Francisco Figueroa, brought the mail up several days a week from the Patagonia post office for a wage of $25 a month. When he passed away, his son Ramon took over. Mrs. Figueroa, who was nursing her son Camilo at the time of the accident, offered to serve as wet nurse. "But I refused. I wanted my bottle," Catherine says.

Josiah was not only a mining engineer, but also a talented poet. He wrote an entire book, "Arizuma," in an off beat cadence known as iambic pentameter. The story told of the Conquistadors' search for a lost vein of ore known as Arizuma that Bond evidently thought might be found in Alto. Although "Arizuma" was published several years before Minnie's death, the dedication is poignantly prophetic:

"With glowing heart, I dedicate this lay to her, my wife!
Who coped with all the hopes and worries of this mountain life,
With patience, constant humor, ready wit and glowing love;
The friendly hostess of all living things;
And hand and glove
With all that's pure and sweet! And may she all the good obtain,
That can be meted out to mortals, and heaven finally gain!"

Josiah Bond wrote "Arizuma" entirely in chant royal, or iambic pentameter, telling the tale of a lost vein of gold. The mining engineer received several awards for his writings and poetry.
Barr photo

Josiah entered a national poetry contest in honor of Admiral Perry, the North Pole explorer. "I remember it well, the day the $50 check came. First prize, awarded to Josiah Bond for his poem entitled 'Perry at the Pole,' a substantial bit of money during the great Depression," a grateful Catherine remembers. "We children were all great readers and used to read his poetry at the table.

"My father served Alto in many ways. He was the justice of the peace. He got the certificates for the new babies, the weddings and even, sadly, for the deaths. After my mother died, he took over as postmaster until the post office closed around 1932 and also served as the schoolteacher for several years.

"The Laguna family, also a large one, lived at Alto for a long time. When Nick Laguna was born Mr. Laguna came to our house to announce his birth, the especially exciting part, he was born on the eleventh day, at the eleventh hour in the eleventh month!

"When my father was on the school board for the Alto School, Mrs. Laguna appealed to him for help. A teacher was trying to get her teenaged son, Alberto, to use his right hand although he was left-handed. My father agreed with her and ordered the teacher to let Alberto be his own normal left-handed self."

Ray Bergier, who also grew up at Alto, remembers Albert (Alberto) Laguna well. "He and I were buddies. We went everywhere together, riding the burros that were used to haul the ore. I remember one time we came down to what they call the Montezuma. It's about halfway between Alto and the creek near Patagonia.

"We wanted to pick some acorns, the Mexicans call them bellotas, they're delicious eating. We saw that a fellow by the name of Jose Soto had gotten to the area before we did and he'd picked a five-gallon can full of acorns and hung it up in a tree. So...we divided it between us.

"As we were heading home, a Model T came along with a bearded old man in the back. He looked like Santa Claus sitting there. He says, 'Boys, boys, come here. Where is the cemetery?' We thought he was trying to find the stolen bucket of acorns, so we answered, 'No hablamos Ingles,' and off we went."

The two youngsters had heard many stories about the nearby Salero Mine, the scene of many Indian raids in the mid-1800s. The mine, just four miles south of Alto, was run by John Wrightston, Gilbert Hopkins, Horace Grosvenor and Raphael Pumpelly. Pumpelly was the only one of the four who was not slain by the Apaches.

The legend was that Pumpelly and Grosvenor had lent some money to a mining company over by Arivaca. Feeling the area was becoming too dangerous they made plans to leave, but when they went to collect their debt the mining company paid them with ore instead of cash.

They loaded a wagon with the ore and hired two Mexicans to drive it back to Salero. When it didn't show up after three or four days, Grosvenor and Pumpelly started out to try and reclaim their property. They had only gone a couple of miles when they saw their wagon coming off the ridge, just south of Josephine Canyon.

"Grosvenor decided to go on ahead and find out what was causing the delay. When he didn't return, Pumpelly rode up on a hill and saw an Apache, all humped up, slipping off down the ridge," said Bergier, enthusiastically recounting the oft-told tale.

It was getting dark by the time Pumpelly made it to the bottom of the canyon and in the dim light, he tripped over Grosvenor's body, which was nearly decapitated by the Indians' lances. The Apaches also killed the two drivers, slaughtered one of the horses, ate it and took the leftovers with them.

Bergier became convinced that the old man he and Albert had seen as kids must have been Raphael Pumpelly, "He went to the graveyard and worked on Grosvenor's grave. It had a nice headstone, but the horses and cattle had knocked it over and he put that back in place. I'm sure it was Pumpelly," Bergier insists, although almost 65 years had passed since the Salero Mine closed in 1865. "He was a really old man."

Bergier remembers Josiah Bond's hope of someday persuading the railroad to run a spur up the mountain to what he steadfastly believed to be a rich vein of ore. Bond penned this verse in tribute to the lowly burro, a beast that despite its penchant for wandering off, was nonetheless invaluable in the early mining days of Arizona:

The Burro
"Without thee, life in passes such as these, would be a grind,
Which even bronco here could not relieve or succor find!
Tis often said that without thee, no mine was ever found,
Because thou coverest minutely every inch of ground;
One prospector tells me he prospected twenty lonesome years,
And of this, spent he hunting burros, with his fears,
Each time aroused that they were gone.
But thou dost never shirk;
I know where'er thou goest, goest but to look for work"

Josiah Bond spent the rest of his life at Alto. He raised his children there, never remarrying, and never giving up on his dreams. His son Albert's wife, Mary Ann Eberling, who became a high school teacher, remembers many evenings discussing the finer points of literature and especially poetry with this literate man who chose to live his life in the remote Santa Rita Mountains.

Josiah Bond, mining engineer, poet, dreamer, husband and father was buried in the family plot beside his beloved wife Minnie on a hillside at Alto September 12, 1938.

Betty Barr

Catherine Bond Elefson was seven months old when she survived the lightning strike that killed her mother. Catherine and her father Josiah Bond. Circa 1936.
Photo courtesy Lucia Bond Konrath.

Catherine Bond Elefson

Alto Camp

Catherine Bond was born February 23, 1922. In the fall of that same year her mother, Minnie, was struck and killed by lightning. Catherine's father, Josiah Bond, was a mining engineer who had brought his young wife to Alto in 1906 where they built their adobe home. The ruins of that home, which also served as Alto's post office, are still standing at the site in the Santa Rita Mountains.

The mine at Alto dates back to the 1690s when the Spanish Jesuits first explored what is now southeastern Arizona. Early legends held that these missionaries discovered the mine, but later historical research does not support that view. A rustic wooden Forest Service sign, since removed from the site, related that tale, along with the information that the mine was deserted during the Apache raids in 1857. The deposits were reclaimed by Mark "Lucky" Lully of Nogales in 1875 and it was then known as the Gold Tree Mine, named for Joseph Goldtree.

The name was later changed to Alto (Spanish for "high") since the diggings, still visible from the townsite, are located on a steep mountainside. The miners came up with an ingenious solution for the hard daily climb. They installed a double set of tracks and utilized cables to run the mine cars up one track and down the other. One man would climb the hill in the morning, load an empty car with waste for ballast and start it on its way down the hill. Several miners at the bottom would jump into an empty car and the weight of the loaded car coming down the hill would pull them up. The car was unloaded at the bottom and used during the day to bring down the ore. When the men were ready to quit for the day their weight, along with the judicious use of the brakes, was enough to bring them back down.

A string of six or eight burros coming down the road from Alto, their pack-saddles loaded with ore, was a familiar sight in Patagonia in those days. On both sides of the track at the Patagonia Depot were big platforms, level with the doors of the train. When the train pulled up to the platforms, the ore would be poured out of the packsaddles directly onto the floor. The silver and lead went to El Paso and the copper went to Douglas. The steadfast burros would then turn around and begin their trip to back to Alto, making the 30-mile roundtrip delivery in one day.

Josiah Bond and his family had lived at Alto for over 16 years when lightning struck, leaving the widower with four children to raise, including the seven-month-old baby. Little Catherine's 12-year-old sister, with the lyrical name of Isabelle Hope Santa Rita Bond, took on the role of her surrogate mother.

Hope would go to school in the morning and brother Albert would stay home and baby-sit. Then he and Hope would trade places for the afternoon session. When Catherine got a little older, she vividly remembers the other children telling her that she would go to the window of the big house and watch for Hope coming home from school. As soon as her sister came into view, Catherine would jump up and down with excitement, saying over and over again, "Hopie, Hopie!"

Minnie Ammerman Bond, the first postmistress at Alto. Circa 1918.
Photo courtesy Lucia Bond Konrath.

34

For two years Josiah took over as teacher at the one-room school in Alto. This was not a position of his choosing, teaching being one of his least favorite activities, but he had a college degree and when the state was not able to find someone for the position he would be pressed into service. In spite of Bond's reluctance, Ray Bergier, one of his pupils, remembers him as one of the best teachers he ever had.

The tiny community boasted a real Sunday school for a short time. Rev. George Wilson, pastor of a Presbyterian church in Tucson, was a missionary-minded man who established Sunday schools at the mining towns of Ruby and Alto. Catherine's oldest brother, Joe, taught the young men's class and her sister Hope also served there. When the old timers began to leave Alto in about 1927, the Sunday school closed. "Counting the young people and all, there were about 18 people left. The Figueroas and Lagunas had big families and then there were the four of us," says Catherine.

By the time Catherine was old enough for school, the state had provided a teacher for the community. There were different teachers over the years and they boarded at Josiah Bond's house. Catherine was the only one of the Bond children to go past eighth grade. "My sister and brothers had all left home by the time I was 13, and it was just me and my dad there until he died about three years later."

An old prospector who made Alto his home until his death in the late '40s, was O. A. Reid. He lived alone in an old adobe house in Josephine Canyon and had his own patented claims. He went into a mineshaft by himself one day, evidently lost his footing and plunged to his death. Rescuers had to go in with bellows to get the polluted air out of the shaft before they could remove his body

"O. A. considered us his family," Catherine says. "He was a lifetime bachelor and we could not find anyone to notify when he died. He ate lunch with us every Sunday for a number of years and told us that he had left a Will, but none was ever found in his neat little adobe house." When O. A. Reid died, he was buried in the Bond's family burial plot above their house. There are no tombstones there, but a stone wall surrounds Josiah and Minnie's graves. Catherine's oldest child, who died at the age of two, is also buried there.

The main Alto Cemetery, on the Baca Float west of Alto, is the burial place of Gilbert Hopkins and John Wrightston, who operated the nearby Salero Mine and were killed by Apaches in the 1850s. The grave of another of their partners, Horace Grosvenor, also massacred by the Indians, is nearby. The two highest peaks in the

Santa Ritas are named for Hopkins and Wrightston. A smaller nearby peak is named for Grosvenor.

After Josiah's death in 1938, Catherine's sister and brother-in-law took her in with them so she could go to high school in Nogales, where they lived. She couldn't afford to go to college and wasn't healthy enough to work her way through, so she took a commercial course which enabled her to get a wartime job in Long Beach after graduation.

Her oldest brother, Joe, was fatally wounded in action during the landing at Normandy. Since their parents had both passed away, Catherine was awarded his insurance in monthly installments of $50. "I also had a little money saved from working in Long Beach, so I returned to the empty home waiting for me at Alto. I moved in and Windsor, my future husband, came to visit. After a brief courtship we were married. "We had known one another for ten years so it was not as sudden as it appeared," Catherine smiles.

Windsor Elefson had come west looking for a job in Superior or Globe during the Depression. He had no previous experience, but got a taste for mining after a trip to Ruby. He met Andrew Bettwy, mayor of Nogales, who leased some of Josiah's claims. He accompanied Bettwy to Alto to meet with Josiah Bond and was introduced to his daughter, Catherine. She was 14 and he was 24. It was ten years before the pair would marry.

The wedding was held at the First Baptist Church in Nogales in 1946. Windsor wore his uniform, although he was no longer in the service, and Catherine was a beautiful bride with blonde, very long hair, and a long train on her dress. The Bergier's hired hand, Ernesto Valenzuela, was their usher and Hope's husband acted as best man.

Catherine and Windsor had a total of nine children. One died young, a son was miscarried and seven children survived. They lived at Alto nine years till the original house, built by her father, burned down to the adobe walls in September 1955.

"We were visiting my sister in Show Low so we, and the four children we had at the time, escaped the fire. My husband had left a big 50-gallon container of gasoline on the truck and we thought that somehow it ignited. The truck was completely burned.

"When Windsor came back to Patagonia people told him, 'Well, you've got nothing left out there.' So he went out there and saw it. The dog that we had left there came creeping over to him; she was scared. Our son, who was three months old when the house burned, remembered when his dad took him back there several years later. They sat together in the truck a long time looking. Our son said, 'I knew it was important, but I didn't know why.'"

After the fire, Windsor finished construction of a frame house he had been building on the edge of the canyon, up above the ruins of the old adobe home. Much of it was finished when the original house burned down, so the displaced family had somewhere to move into. Sadly, it was to be for a short time. "We lived there for a while but the Forest Service tore it down and threw our windows in the canyon. Most of it was Forest Service land.

"I sold the old home place to my niece because I needed the money…to salvage the mining claims. We saved ten claims that way. I still have patented claims too. My father bought a good many claims. Some of them went up for tax sale, but I have the rest."

"We were the last to leave Alto," Catherine mourns as she remembers that none of the other families were still living there when she and Windsor packed up their family and belongings for the last time. They lived in Sonoita for 17 years and eventually bought a house in Huachuca City, where Catherine still lives. Windsor died in 1984 and is buried in the Fruitland Cemetery in Sonoita.

Today purple and white irises dot the hillsides around Alto. "My mother planted them when she would go riding up in the hills on her horse. My sister and I divided them and planted lots more of them. You will still find them in odd places in the area," Catherine remembers.

Each spring the iris bulbs planted by Minnie Bond so long ago resiliently poke their heads through the rocky soil. Their blooms sway in the breeze, softening the starkness of the crumbling walls of the home that Josiah built more than a century ago and painting a visual reminder of a town that is no more.

Crumbling adobe ruins of the Alto Post Office, established June 6, 1912. Ray Bergier's home was about one mile away, just over the hill rising in the background.
Barr photo.

Ray Bergier

Alto

The year was 1916, the State of Arizona was a mere four years old, and "wild west" was still a pretty good description of life in southeastern Arizona. It was a day in early March when Bob Bergier and his wife, Willie, boarded the train that passed through Patagonia every morning. They were off to visit his sister who had a place down on Sonoita Creek. On the return trip, "My mother went into labor and they didn't think she could make it to Patagonia on the train, so she got off at the Gatlin's place (what is now the Circle Z Guest Ranch) and I was born there," Ray Bergier explains with a chuckle. And so began what was to be Ray's journey of a lifetime.

Willie Florence Chapman Bergier had arrived in Arizona around 1906 by way of Las Vegas, New Mexico, where her family ran cattle. Hoping to find a better place to live, they sent her uncle, Al Chapman, to check out southeastern Arizona. "He was a little guy. Didn't weigh nothing, but he could herd horses back quicker than anybody. On the first day out he sore-backed the old mare and hated to ride her 300 miles or whatever. So he saw a big old gray burro and he roped it, saddled it and rode it down here." The journey took six days and Uncle Al liked what he saw. The family loaded their cattle on the train and drove their horses through Clifton and down to the Mowry area where they first settled. Years later, Ray rode that same burro to school for almost four years.

Ray's father, Bob Bergier, arrived by a different route. He was born and raised in Idaho where his family had a farm and raised dairy cattle. At the age of 12 he would get up early, go down to the creek with an ax and chop a hole in the ice for the cattle to drink. The Bergiers supplied milk and cream to the big hotel at a nearby ski resort. The manager offered to pay young Bob .05 or .06 cents for every trout he could catch. Bob would chop the ice hole, catch a few fish and throw them out on the cold ground where they would immediately freeze. Later he would send the trout to the hotel along with the milk and cream. To make matters even better, his dad told him that when he had $5 collected, he would "get him a heifer".

A war between the local cattle ranchers and sheepherders caused the family to relocate to Canelo in 1900. By that time young Bob had five heifers that he branded with the Bar R. That was the be-

ginning of the cattle business that they still have today. The Bergier family acquired another brand, the KZ, at a later date.

The young family lived at the Ranger Station at Temporal until Ray was about six years old. Ray remembers when his dad bought the Alto rangelands from his father-in-law, "Old Pat Ferris came with his wagon and loaded everything up and hauled it up to the mountain." Today, there is nothing to mark the town of Alto but the crumbling ruins of the old adobe post office. A Forest Service sign marking the spot where the post office was established June 6, 1912 has succumbed to the ravages of time and is no longer there.

Forest Service sign pictured at Alto Camp in 2000, has since fallen over and been removed. The sign stated that mineral deposits were first discovered in the area by Jesuit priests of the Tumacacori Mission in 1687. Recent discoveries have contradicted this version.
Barr photo.

In 1922 there was still a lot of activity in Alto, although the mine was no longer profitable and many people had started moving away before Ray and his family arrived. Josiah Bond, whose wife had been the first postmistress, taught at the two-room school there.

Willie Bergier's days were full. Early in the morning she would go out on the roundups because she was the only one her husband trusted to bring the cattle in calmly enough so that their tongues wouldn't be hanging out. After that, she would come home and fix dinner and do all the chores usually relegated to women. One day the whole family was helping out at the old ranch owned by Bird Yoas, their neighbor to the west. During the roundup, Bird came over to Willie and asked if she would send young Ray to the breezeway where Yoas had a sack of jerky. "Raymond can pound that up and you can make us some jerky gravy," he said. The gravy was excellent so the next day Bird asked them to make up another batch.

Ray was banging away on the jerky when Bird showed up and yelled, "Oh no, don't use that. That's my horse jerky that I use to feed the dogs." Ray thought that over after Bird left, and considering all the effort he had just expended on filling a whole pan full of jerky, he decided to continue with his pounding. According to his best recollection, the resulting gravy was just as good as the first batch. "I don't know if the horse died accidentally or they killed it or what, but we ate the gravy and it was good," Ray says.

Their living quarters were an old miner's shack made of tin and very little lumber. It was hard to get to town and they only made four or five trips a year. At tax time, Willie rode the 15 miles to Patagonia where she could catch the train to get to the Nogales Courthouse. By the time she got to town the train had already left, so she set out for home. She soon discovered to her dismay that she had lost the $35 tax money and figured that some people she had passed on the road must have found it. When she arrived back in Patagonia she found the men drunk in the bar and the money gone. "It took my dad three months doing everything he could think of to get the $35 to pay the taxes," Ray says.

Ray's father bought a large portion of the Baca Float Ranch in 1945 for $10 an acre. According to Ray, "Everybody thought he was a damn fool." Mr. Gatlin, the postmaster, told Bob Bergier, "I hear you've gone wild and paid $10 an acre for your land. I have 1,100 acres I want to sell you." Bergier told him to get it ready and he bought it then and there. About a year later Gatlin handed him a check for $11,000 and said, "I decided you don't need the ranch. I'll just take it back." Bergier cheerfully declined that offer.

The Figueroa family was paid $25 a month to haul the mail back and forth to Alto three days a week, by any kind of transport they could arrange – horseback, an old wagon or a buggy. That job gave them enough money for beans and tortillas, a delicacy for Ray whose mother didn't know how to prepare Mexican food. At lunch recess, Ray would run about 200 yards from the school up to the Figueroa house and trade Mrs. Figueroa his lunch of sandwiches, cookies and cake for beans and tortillas. "We were both happy," Ray remembers with a smile.

Ray picked up three really nice lion dogs that were turned loose at the high school because no one wanted them. When he arrived home with three extra dogs his dad was pretty upset since they already had about four of their own, but after a successful coon hunt he relented and grudgingly let Ray keep them. In the fall when there was a little snow on the ground, Ray and a friend saddled up and rode to the cut between Baldy and Hopkins and ran into a lion eating a deer in the middle of the trail. On the way home with their trophy, their dogs treed a bobcat and they got that too.

The Opera House at Patagonia was the scene of many community productions. Ray Bergier's parents were attending a show here when Ray and his friend interrupted them to show off the mountain lion and bobcat captured with the help of their new hound dogs.
Photo courtesy Bowman Archives Room.

Back in Patagonia, Ray's parents were at a show at the Opera House and that same night the high school was having a basketball game. When the elder Bergier saw what the boys had, he walked over to the ballgame pulling the lion and bobcat behind him and said to the crowd, "My boys caught these lions with my hounds."

For the next ten years "his hounds" were successful in helping to get lions off the mountain on a regular basis.

Many years have passed since Willie Bergier's memorable train ride. The trains and even the tracks are long gone. It should come as no surprise that Ray Bergier along with Henrietta Taylor, another community leader, made the presentation to Southern Pacific that resulted in the company donating the property for the Town of Patagonia Park.

Betty Barr

Mary Ann Eberling. Circa 1938.
Photo courtesy Lucia Bond Konrath.

Mary Ann Eberling

Canelo and Patagonia

"My grandmother was a wanderer," says Lucia Bond Konrath. "You never could fence her in, even when she was a little child."

As a child of three, she was wandering around the desert area near their home in Altar, Mexico. Her father worked there for Tom Heady, foreman of the Greene Cattle Company, which had ranches on both sides of the border. The Seri Indians had demanded that Heady provide them with a calf to feed their hungry tribe, but he refused and the Indians captured little Mary Ann as ransom for their demands. Heady remained steadfast, but after three days, John Eberling, Mary Ann's father, refused to do any further work on the ranch until his daughter was rescued and Heady was forced to relent.

Mary Ann says that the Mexicans had banished the Indians from Tiburon, their native island territory. Because of this, the Seris hated the Mexicans and refused to speak Spanish. They had learned English however, so she could understand what they were saying. They took Mary Ann to a large wash where the men of the tribe began digging a pit in the sand. She asked the tribal children why they were building a big fire in the pit and they told her they were preparing a bed for her. Remembering stories about the cannibal Seris, the little girl suddenly feared that they were going to roast her for their dinner.

The Seris were not interested in roasting their captive white child, however. Instead, they shoveled the hot coals out of the fire pit and laid their own children, as well as Mary Ann, into the depression that was left. They piled the hot sand over the children, covering them up to their necks, and then put the hot rocks back on top of the sand to keep them warm during the night.

The next morning, they served giant sea turtle eggs for breakfast. The eggs had a tough leathery outer skin. The Indians cut a slit in the skin and poured the raw egg directly into their mouths. The little girl was repulsed and refused to partake of this feast.

Since there was no meat to sustain them, they caught a burro. The men ran circles around the beast until he dropped of exhaustion, then they slit his throat with a sharp seashell and caught the blood in a turtle shell that was passed around for everyone to share. The meat was roasted briefly and eaten partially raw. Giant tortoise shells served as bowls and cooking utensils.

After American businesses were forced out of Mexico, Heady moved the cattle operations to the Greene Cattle Company's American headquarters at the San Rafael Ranch in Lochiel, Arizona, where he continued as foreman. Mary Ann's father was a cowboy on the ranch and one of the only people who could handle their wild stallion.

When Mary Ann was about five years old, Eberling was shoeing the stallion in the barn. Always a free spirit, the little girl was up in the hayloft gathering spider webs for the upcoming roundup. There were lots of black widows and daddy long legs in the barn and the sticky webs came in handy to staunch the flow of blood after the dehorning at the roundups. Mary Ann would plunge a long stick into the webs and twist it round and round until she had a good supply of the sticky stuff. She was blithely unconcerned about the possibility of poisonous spider bites.

Down on the floor of the barn John Eberling had just started pounding a nail into the hoof of the stallion when a cowboy came up to the doorway and shouted a greeting. The startled horse spooked and lashed out with his rear leg, slashing Eberling across his belly with the half exposed nail. The deep wound extended from one side of his stomach to the other. He was critically injured and in extreme pain.

Little Mary Ann raced down from the hayloft and fled toward the house to get Mr. Heady. Mary Ann spent most of her time with Heady's parents, who were deaf and spoke only German. Consequently she not only was fluent in German but spoke very loudly as a child. Her multilingual father spoke French and English as well as

Spanish and German, but her Mexican mother spoke only Spanish. Ironically she could not convey the disastrous news to her mother because at that time, Mary Ann spoke mostly German.

Heady could understand what the terrified child was saying however, and he hurried to the barn, grabbed a sheet and wrapped it tightly around Eberling's midsection. They drove all the way to St. Joseph's Hospital in Nogales in his Model T Ford. It was the only car in the county and good transportation; nevertheless, it was a long and painful trip. Eventually Eberling recovered from his injuries enough to be discharged, but his cowboying days were numbered. He could never ride a horse or even stand completely upright again. He and his wife and growing family of ten children moved to Vaughn and later Canelo where they eked out a living as sharecroppers.

Teacher Henrietta Martin in the doorway of the Canelo one-room school. Standing in front of the teacher, at the middle of the photo from left to right are: Frances Eberling, Emma Lou Pyeatt, Pauline and Margaret Eberling. The three little boys at the right end of the front row are Clarence, Johnny and Joe Eberling. The other children have not been identified. Circa mid-1930s.
Photo courtesy Lucia Bond Konrath.

Mary Ann attended the first three grades at the one-room Vaughn School near Elgin and then went to live with her father's sister, Eva, in the Los Angeles area. She attended school there through the eighth grade. By this time, Mary Ann's love of education had crystallized. She would be a student of literature and a dedicated reader for the rest of her life.

She returned to Arizona every summer to help the family with the farm, but her first love remained her studies. After eighth grade the Great Depression hit and her aunt and uncle left the Los Angeles area and returned to Tubac to raise crops. Mary Ann moved back with her parents who were now farming in Canelo. She attended the one-room school there for a year.

In 1934 she got permission from the authorities to work her way through Patagonia Union High School. Child labor laws prevented her from taking an actual job, but the judge ruled that she could leave school one hour early and work for her room and board at a local boarding house. She got a job with Mrs. Parten who ran Casa Vieja, a boarding house for teachers located across the bridge just north of town. She worked from 3:30 to 11 p.m. There was no room for her to sleep there, so she paid Mrs. Costello $10 a month to board at her house in town.

A young man named Albert Bond worked at the light company, just across the road from the Casa Vieja. Tramps would cook their stolen chickens and corn under the bridge, so to protect her, Albert would walk her home after work. If he couldn't get off in time, Howard Easley, who worked at the Wagon Wheel, would come for her. Albert was a little jealous when Howard was walking Mary Ann home, so he would hide under the bridge and pretend to be a troll to scare her.

In 1940 Mary Ann and Albert Bond were married. Albert was the son of Josiah Bond, a mining engineer who ran an assay company at Alto Camp in the Santa Rita Mountains. Josiah's wife, Minnie, was the first postmistress at Alto. When Albert was only 14 years old, he and his mother were out riding when a sudden storm came up and she was struck and killed by lightning.

Young Albert was so traumatized that he didn't speak for three years after the tragedy. Minnie had been carrying her seven-month old daughter, Catherine, on the saddle with her. At the first sign of the storm, she wrapped the baby in a slicker and blanket. The bolt of lightning that killed Minnie knocked little Catherine to the ground and her life was spared. Albert did not speak for a long time after the accident.

Albert and Mary Ann Eberling Bond with son Eddie in her arms. From left are children, Phil, David and Charlotte. Mary Ann still lives in this house that Albert built in Double Adobe around 1948.

Photo courtesy of Lucia Bond Konrath

Mary Ann received her teaching certificate from Arizona State University in 1940 and she and her new husband moved to Arkansas where they thought the lower elevation would be good for his heart condition. In spite of his poor health Albert was drafted in the Second World War because he had an engineering degree and was needed in the Corps of Engineers. He was stationed in the Aleutians. Mary Ann remained in Arkansas during the war and taught at the one-room Hills Chapel School in Hope, Arkansas (birthplace of President Clinton) from 1944 - 45.

After the war the couple moved back to Arizona and Alfred built the home in Double Adobe, between Bisbee and Douglas, where Mary Ann has lived for almost 60 years. She taught at one-room schools in Double Adobe and at Wonderland of Rocks in the Chiricahuas. She retired after a 37-year teaching career, 24 of them as the English and Spanish teacher at Bisbee High School. Albert died of a heart attack in 1967 and several years later Mary Ann married Junior Fairchild. "I was fortunate to find the two best husbands in the world," she says.

Ironically, when Mary Ann graduated from Patagonia Union High School, Tom Heady was on the school board and presented the diplomas to the graduating seniors in her class. He had this to say about Mary Ann: "She had an eye for quality even at an early age. When she was five years old she came into the store on the San Rafael Ranch with a little puppy. We had a prize bull and I had told her father to take good care of him because he had a pedigree as long as your arm. Well, Mary

Ann came in and I told her, 'Kid, you got a nice dog there,' and she says to me, "He's got a pedigree as long as your arm."

Mary Ann's children, grandchildren, and many devoted students are convinced that she too has a pedigree as long as your arm.

Dwayne and Zalia Rogers
HC 1 Box 7
76 Mustang Ranch Road
Elgin, AZ 85611-9702

Betty Barr

Mark and Nellie Bartlett didn't let circumstances dictate their style. Even while living in a tent Nellie set a formal table, complete with linen, fine dishes, silverware and crystal. Circa 1912. Photo courtesy Marka Moss and Jane Woods

Marcus and Nellie Bartlett
Chopeta and Fern Bartlett Collie

Elgin

When Marcus, "Mark," Bartlett was only 15 years old, his uncle sold him into the army for $50. During the Civil War, it was a rather common practice for unscrupulous men to pocket the enlistment bonus and then coerce someone to take their place with a vague promise to repay when the war was over. Young Mark ended up as a bugler with McClellan's Army, 6th Cavalry, Company B, Ohio. He never collected the $50.

Conditions at the front were abominable. Poor nutrition and sanitation caused many soldiers to fall ill even if they were not wounded, and Mark was no exception. He contracted what was probably typhoid fever and was loaded into a boxcar full of the sick and wounded for transport away from the battlefields. The overcrowded boxcar was stranded on a sidetrack for days and Mark was one of the few to survive the ordeal. When his fever finally broke, his crop of flaming red hair fell out, only to grow back in a dull brown. He remained in frail health for the rest of his life.

After the Civil War, Mark went west for a time and lived with the Indians in Minnesota. Following a divorce, he returned to his hometown of Brecksville, near Cleveland, and met Nellie, an unmarried woman in her late thirties. Nellie and Mark were soon married, although according to their granddaughters, Marka Moss and

Jane Woods, it was quite scandalous in those days for their grandmother to marry a divorced man.

Nellie was over 40 when the Bartlett daughters were born, Chopeta Lewis Bartlett in 1892 and Alice Fern Bartlett in 1894. Chopeta was named for a well-known Indian maiden that her father had heard about during his time in Minnesota.

Bartlett was an electrician and their home in Brecksville was one of the few in town to boast of electric lights. The neighborhood children loved to come over to watch the magic of the lights coming on when he flicked the switches.

By 1912 Bartlett's health had deteriorated badly and he decided that the only hope for a cure was to move west. He loaded up a boxcar with all the family's furniture and belongings, including their milk cow, and rode with it to Arizona. Nellie and her daughters traveled the same route by passenger train.

The minute 17-year-old Fern stepped off the train at the Elgin Depot in Arizona, Stone Collie spotted her. He was one of the local boys who found it great sport to meet the arriving train every day and check out the newcomers, many of them survivors of the Civil War who came west to claim homesteads. Stone boldly introduced himself to Fern and invited her to a dance that very evening at the local hotel (which has long since

Nellie Bartlett was over 40 years old when her daughters, Fern (left) and Chopeta were born in 1894 and 1892, respectively. Circa 1896.
Photo courtesy Marka Moss and Jane Woods.

burned down). Despite the fact that they were strict parents, Mark and Nellie said, "Yes," to this young man whom they had never seen before.

The Bartletts immediately set about "proving up" a 160-acre homestead in Elgin on the same parcel where their granddaughters, Jane Woods and Marka Moss, and Marka's husband Austin, still live today. Nellie Bartlett was a very proper woman and felt it was important to maintain her high standards no matter what the situation. Dinner was a formal affair, even while the family was living in a tent. Meals were a sit-down affair; the table set with linen, crystal, china dishes and silverware.

Jane remembers Grandmother Bartlett's way of handling unwanted traveling salesmen, "Grandma would come to the door and tell the peddler firmly, 'NO thank you,' and he would never dare to return."

The Bartletts arrived in Elgin in the month of May, but the climate was not enough to fight off Mark's illness. By the following October he passed away. By then Chopeta had met and promised to marry Bill Collie, Stone's older brother. The new widow didn't want to go back to Ohio and leave her soon-to-be-married daughter behind, so the three women stayed on.

To survive after Bartlett's death, Nellie was required to plant 40 acres of the 160-acre homestead or risk losing it. This worked well for the first few years, when the rains were plentiful. The women were able to dry farm by planting beans and other crops that didn't require much water. After the drought, dry farming was no longer an option, and Nellie supplemented their income by taking in foster children.

As a veteran's widow, Nellie received a small pension and was eligible to homestead an additional 160 acres. She added to her holdings by buying a relinquishment - a parcel that the homesteader was not able to keep either because he couldn't "prove up," or got discouraged and left. The relinquishment was on a beautiful site directly north of her existing acreage, the current home of Pat and Wayne Basinger. That is the site where Nellie chose to build her house. Eventually she amassed 1,000 acres, and rented out the pasturage to other ranchers for cattle grazing.

The Bartletts became close friends of the neighboring Collie family. Chopeta Bartlett, who had attended Oberlin Music Institute in Ohio, was a very accomplished pianist and Fern played violin as well as piano. Their big square grand piano had come to Arizona in the boxcar, alongside the furniture and the milk cow. Stone, Bill and Dixie Collie all loved to sing and the young friends spent many evenings harmonizing at the Bartlett home while Fern and Chopeta played.

Chopeta soon qualified for her teaching certificate and her first assignment was in the San Rafael Valley. After that, she taught at the one-room school in Rain Valley. When she and Bill Collie were married she went to live on his homestead in the Vaughn area.

Fern taught at the Evans School at a mining camp in Lyle Canyon for two years. She was then named the first schoolteacher at newly-built Canelo School. She boarded with a local family during the week and rode her horse home to Elgin to spend the weekends with her mother. Her friend Stone was a tall, handsome young fellow but Fern was still young and in the intervening years before their wedding, she became engaged and then unengaged to another suitor. She finally agreed to marry Stone about seven years after their first meeting.

Stone's sister, Dixie, and Fern had become the best of friends and when both became engaged at about the same time it was only natural that they would share

Almond and Dixie Walker (from left) and Dixie's brother, Stone Collie and Fern Bartlett, were married in a double wedding, August 28, 1919, at Nellie Bartlett's homestead in Elgin. Stone's brother, Bill, had married Fern's sister, Chopeta, several years previously and their daughter, Leslie, was the flower girl.
Photo courtesy Marka Moss and Jane Woods.

their wedding day. Stone and Fern Bartlett Collie and Almond and Dixie Collie Walker had a double wedding August 28, 1919 at Nellie Bartlett's homestead in Elgin. Bill and Chopeta Bartlett Collie's little girl, Leslie, was a flower girl.

Dixie had met Almond Walker when she was teaching at the mining community of Russellville, near Dragoon. She boarded at the C Bar Ranch, a large cattle ranch owned by Fred Fiegge that employed several cowboys. According to Dixie's memoirs, "One cowboy was Almond E. Walker. He was very handsome and we soon became sweethearts."

Not long after their marriage the couple experienced life-threatening troubles. Almond developed pleurisy and his wife was hard pressed to care for her sick husband with a toddler, a new baby on the way and no income. Mr. Peacock, a part owner of the C Bar, as well as a lawyer, took them under his wing and with his help they were able to get the compensation they were due from Almond's disability discharge.

Dixie said, "Mr. Peacock went to work and before too long a government check was coming each month but we did not collect for all the years that we received nothing. Some of it finally came after a long wait. Many times I would have only ten or twenty cents in my purse. It almost seemed like someone had his arm around us when a check would come in the mail."

Meanwhile, Stone and Fern had been running cattle on their homestead when cattle prices bombed in 1925. They had shipped an entire trainload of cows to California and only received $12 a head for them. The Collies, along with their first child, Marka, and Grandma Nellie Bartlett, moved to Tucson where Stone found work as a journeyman carpenter. Stone eventually sold his homestead near Vaughn, but Grandma Bartlett still kept her properties in Elgin

The family lived on Campbell Avenue out by the University of Arizona farms, and had a riding stable on the property where they gave lessons to winter visitors. Their second daughter, Jane, was born while they lived in Tucson. By 1937 Stone had tired of carpentry work and city life and wanted to return to the ranch. The family moved into the old Bartlett homestead, renamed it Mustang Ranch, and opened it as a dude ranch.

The original house was constructed of adobe, with very thick walls that kept it cool in summer and warm in winter. Stone hauled rocks from all over the property and started covering the outside walls of the house, adding mortar as he went along. The final result is the beautiful rock house that Pat and Wayne Basinger live in today. Collie became well known for his rock building skills, and years later built the stone fireplace in the Elgin Club.

Grandma Bartlett died a year after the Collies moved back to the ranch. She and her husband are buried in the Bartlett plot in Brecksville, Ohio. Years later, their granddaughter Marka made a trip to Ohio during Memorial Day weekend and was honored to be invited, in a very emotional ceremony, to place a wreath on her grandfather's grave in the veteran's section of the cemetery.

While they were operating the guest ranch, Stone picked up a horse named Old Blue. He asked his brother-in-law Almond Walker, who broke many horses and was a good bronc rider, for advice on his purchase. Almond judged the horse mean and said it wouldn't make a good dude horse. He added, "If you are really tough on him he will just put his head between his front legs and buck until you go off, but if you treat him gentle, he might be okay to ride."

Stone decided to keep the animal and Old Blue became his favorite riding horse, in spite of the fact that he bucked him off many times. He was even able to put guests up on Old Blue with no problem. One day however, Fern and daughter Jane were going out riding together and when Jane saddled up Old Blue, before she even got fully seated, he got his head down. Jane says they went charging and bucking across the pasture and all she could think of was how many times her dad had gone off him. "I thought to myself, if Dad couldn't stay on him, there's no way I'm going to, and I didn't."

When Fern was in the hospital for many days with pneumonia, the family was forced to sell some horses to pay the medical bills. Emory Stoddard, who traded in horses and cattle, came to the house and loaded up Son-of-a-Gun and Old Blue in his trailer. Daughter Jane remembers, "Son-of-a-Gun loaded in and never looked back. Old Blue was facing forwards as they drove out the driveway. Just as they left, he turned his head and looked reproachfully at me and Dad."

Captain Stone and Fern Collie are buried at Black Oak Pioneer Cemetery. Their daughters, Marka Moss and Jane Woods still live on adjoining parcels on Grandma Nellie Bartlett's original homestead in Elgin. A third daughter, Faye Miller, lives in Ajo.

Betty Barr

The Elgin Store slogan was, "Elgin, where the sun shines and wind blows." Seated on the bench are Stone Collie and Russell Van Gorder. On horseback from the rear are, Marka Collie (Moss), Faye Collie (Miller) and Mr. Braun.
Photo courtesy Jane Woods and Marka Moss and the Bowman Archives Center.

Ruben and Lucinda Collie
Stone Collie and Dixie Collie Walker

Elgin

Captain Stone Collie was the 12th of Ruben and Lucinda Collie's 13 children. "I guess his parents ran out of names by the time he came along," his daughter, Marka Moss, chuckles, "so they named him for Captain Stone, a military man they admired." Collie enlisted in the cavalry in World War I, but since the regiment at nearby Fort Huachuca was an all-black "Buffalo Soldiers" unit, he was sent to a camp in Douglas where his unusual first name was destined to cause him a few hassles.

The young private was eagerly anticipating a promised box of homemade cookies from his mother, and the wait seemed endless. Finally, he discovered that Lucinda had addressed the coveted package to "Captain Stone Collie," and it had been routed through the officers' quarters, much to the delight of said officers. Private Collie complained that by the time the box got to the enlisted men's barracks the cookies were half gone or stale. He had to make do with the few crumbs that were left.

Stone's sister Dixie remembered, "Stone and Jim Yeary, our soldier boys from Elgin, were homesick. Fern (Fern Bartlett, Stone's future wife) and I went to Douglas to visit them one weekend. We wore new taffeta dresses, very fashionable then, and the new high-top shoes."

Collie served all his time at the Douglas camp, training men for the cavalry and attaining the rank of corporal. According to his daughter, Jane Woods, he was disappointed that the only action he saw was chasing Pancho Villa across the border into Mexico.

Stone and Dixie's parents, Ruben and Lucinda Collie, originally from Kentucky, had come to Elgin in 1908, after living five years in Dallas. Lucinda was suffering from what she referred to as "the rheumatiz." Little was known about remedies for arthritis at that time, so when they heard from another son, Bill, who was already homesteading in the area, that the dry Arizona climate would be beneficial for his mother's health, they came out to investigate.

Their son, Bill, had learned of homesteading opportunities in Arizona in a roundabout way. While he was working construction in Dallas he ran into a fast-talking man named Tom Wills who regaled the impressionable young man with tales of his huge ranch in beautiful southeastern Arizona. Before long Collie packed up his belongings and headed west.

When Collie asked around Elgin about the important rancher, Mr. Wills, people were either surprised or bewildered. It seemed that Wills lived in a small shack on someone else's property in upper Lyle Canyon in the Huachuca Mountains. He did a little prospecting and brewed moonshine to scratch out a living. From time to time Wills would disappear and return with his pockets full of money. On one occasion he reportedly arrived in Elgin in a big fancy car waving around wads of cash.

The source of his sudden bursts of wealth turned out to be the product of his glib tongue. Wills was selling shares in non-existent land to gullible people enthralled with the romance of the West. When his unsuspecting "clients" arrived to claim their new property, they found their papers were worthless. The wily con artist lived in such a remote area that his victims never could get in touch with him and get their money back.

The Collies were not taken in by Wills' claims, but they loved the rolling hill country of Elgin and filed an application to homestead on 160 acres at the headwaters of the Babocamari creek, just south of the present-day Elgin Club. They dug a well by hand and constructed an adobe house from clay found on the property.

At that time the mail would arrive at the Elgin train depot and travel by horse or wagon ten miles to the post office at Canille (now called Canelo). Elgin residents had to make the roundtrip to Canille to pick up their mail. Ruben successfully petitioned to have a post office located more conveniently at Elgin, and became the first postmaster there on February 12, 1910, two years before Arizona attained statehood.

Lucinda's health continued to improve and she became active again. Feeling that she still needed help, Ruben built a frame building for the post office adjacent to their adobe house so he could be nearby. In one part of the post office, he carried staples and canned goods for sale.

Stone Collie in bow tie and bare feet at about the age of ten. Circa 1902.
Photo courtesy Marka Moss and Jane Woods.

Most of Ruben and Lucinda's children were married by the time the couple moved to Arizona, but they soon sent for young Stone and his sister Dixie, who had been living with siblings in Texas. In her memoirs, Dixie recounted her first sight of Arizona.

"We had to change in Benson, Arizona, to the train that ran to Nogales, which is on the Mexican/U.S. border. We arrived at Elgin in the afternoon. I fell in love with Arizona the minute I left the train. I'd never seen anything as beautiful. The entire country was green as far as one could see. There had been good rains all summer and the grass was plentiful. Looking south were the Canelo Hills, on the west the Santa Rita Mountains, to the south the Huachucas, and northeast the Whetstones. It was a huge valley and there were no fences except small fenced-in plots and the railroad.

"The country was wide open. One could strike out and go straight to any place in the valley. There were a few roads. One went to Canelo and (another) to Nogales that more or less followed the railroad track. On the way to Nogales there were the stations called Sonoita and Patagonia."

Stone Collie was only 18 years old at the time, but he applied for a homestead near brother Bill's place in the Vaughn area. To legally prove up a homestead a person had to be 21 years of age, so another one of his sisters moved to Arizona and lived with him until the paperwork was done.

Dixie, who was two years younger than Stone, loved her father's iron-gray mare, Kitty, which she rode all over exploring the countryside. There wasn't much in the way of entertainment for young people, but they did hold cowboy dances. Dixie said, "My parents frowned on dancing, but Stone, Bill and I went anyway and before long they were going along with us."

The Vaughn Church after a snowfall in the late 1920s. The foundations of the building are barely visible near the site of the old town of Vaughn, where Ruben and Fern first set up housekeeping. Photo courtesy Ilene Fraizer.

Dixie and Fern Bartlett (Stone's future wife) went to Flagstaff together to earn their teaching certificates. Dixie's first assignment was at Mowry, a closed-down mining community. A caretaker looked after the company's holdings and many miners were still living there and working at nearby mines. Dixie recalled, "There were about 30 children, all Mexican, except one little towheaded American boy about eight years old."

Mowry is 30 miles from Elgin and the only transportation was by horseback, so Dixie bought a saddle and a dependable pony, pure white, and together they covered many miles. Mr. Phelps was the storekeeper, and Dixie rented a tent house across the road from his home. The sides and floor of a tent-house are made of lumber and the tent is stretched over a frame. It boasts a real door, not a tent flap. The stove that heated the room also had a flat top for cooking.

"I was very excited about teaching, but I also had many doubts about my ability. There were children from (ages) six to 16...three or four grades. A few children could speak English and were a big help in teaching the others who only spoke Spanish.

"Everything went on routinely until one day a little girl was absent. I asked her sister why she had not come to school. She replied in Spanish, 'No esta aqui.' It sounded to me like she said she had no stockings. What she said was, "She isn't here." At noon I bought a pair of stockings at the store and gave them to her sister. The children were hilarious (sic) over my mistake."

The following year Dixie taught at Greaterville, another mining town, where she was paid an additional $5 per month. Mowry was an underground mine, but Greaterville was a placer mine where the miners dug shallow holes down to loose gravel and sifted the gravel to find flecks or nuggets of gold. The area was worked over but there were still enough miners and their families that a school was needed.

All the dwellings were small one-room adobes with roofs thatched with bear grass. There was no place for Dixie to board so her brother Bill went to Nogales and bought lumber to construct a one-room shack for her to live in, near Mr. Pfiffer's store, and a corral for her horse. When school got out at 4 p.m. on Friday, Dixie would mount up and ride the 25 miles from Greaterville to Elgin to spend the weekend with her parents. She said, "It would be dark before I could ride that far. Sometimes I was really scared. In the dark the yucca plants took on many frightening shapes. Over the weekend I was able to help my parents bake bread and do the laundry."

Late one night Dixie was awakened by someone trying to force open her door. She grabbed the pistol Bill had given her and when the person continued pounding, all the while mumbling incoherently, she pointed toward the door and pulled the trigger. Dixie had shot Mr. Pfiffer, the storekeeper, who was drunk and had mistaken her house for the outhouse. "I had shot him in the side, low down, but the bullet pierced his lung and came out his back. Fortunately, there were two or three men at the store playing poker and they took him to Tucson to a doctor." Although Dixie's memoirs indicate that Mr. Pfiffer recovered from his wounds, most accounts of the day say that he did not survive. He is reported to have avowed on his deathbed that the shooting was his own fault. He had warned the teacher to never let anyone in the door after dark.

Carl Schofield, the Forest Ranger at Rosemont, offered to have Dixie board with him, his wife and two small girls. After she took a week off to recover from the trauma of the shooting, Dixie moved in with them and finished the school term. She rode five miles roundtrip to school every day and 25 miles and back to Elgin every weekend for the rest of that term, all the while outfitted in a divided skirt as it was considered immodest to wear pants. "Everyone conformed to custom no matter how cumbersome," Dixie recalled.

By 1919 Bill, Stone and Dixie had all married. Their mother's arthritis had flared up again and was now a chronic problem. When their sister, Evangeline, invited her parents to come live with her family in Dallas, Ruben sold his homestead and their few cattle and horses and they went to Texas, where he and Lucinda lived out the rest of their years.

Dixie Collie and her husband Almond Walker eventually moved to Tucson where they farmed and operated a chicken ranch. Brothers Bill and Stone Collie married sisters Chopeta and Fern Bartlett and became important and respected members of the growing Sonoita/Elgin community.

Betty Barr

The Canelo one-room school first opened its doors in September, 1912.
Barr photo.

Canelo one-room schoolhouse

The Canelo School opened its door for the first time September 1912. Approximately 30 scrubbed and eager faces sought their first glimpse of the teacher. In stepped twenty-year old, Miss Fern Bartlett, a petite young girl dressed in a voluminous skirt divided so she could ride her horse to school without a sidesaddle, and looking deceptively lenient to their young eyes. Behind her pretty exterior was an elegant but firm disciplinarian who had no trouble at all in controlling this large group of children ranging in age from first to eighth graders. That first class was made up of many names still familiar in the area including the Pyeatt, Bowers, Parker, Eason, Federico and Gonzales families.

Elgin residents Marka Moss and Jane Woods are Fern Bartlett Collie's daughters. They remember their mother telling how she got her teaching certificate at Northern Arizona University Teaching College and came back to Elgin to live with her widowed mother. She rode her horse cross-country to Canelo every Monday morning, a distance of about 8 miles. She would arrive several hours before school began so that she could sweep out, start a fire in the wood burning stove, draw water from the well with a rope and bucket and prepare her lessons for the day. She boarded with local families like the Parkers or Bowers during the week and rode her horse home to Elgin on Fridays to spend the weekends with her mother.

School began with the raising of the flag and Pledge of Allegiance. The day was dedicated almost entirely to learning the basics, with patriotism and American history strongly emphasized. There were no extra curricular activities as we know them today; even 4-H was unheard of. However, there was a piano at the school, and Fern was an accomplished musician who also played the violin. There were music recitals, and special programs were put on for holidays and other occasions.

The children were divided into groups, the older ones helping the younger. One of Fern's students was Byrd Lindsey's mother, Eunice Parker. Eunice was the same age as Fern and they were the best of friends. Eunice could have gone to Tombstone to high school as most of the children in the area did, but was a whiz at algebra and wanted to learn from her friend Fern, so she stayed on at the Canelo School. Another older student was a 22-year-old man who desperately wanted to learn to read and write.

One day during recess, some children smacked a bullet on a rock, and in the ensuing explosion a child lost a finger. Teachers had to rely on their own resources in time of trouble. Fern provided emergency care and calmed the other students for many hours until help arrived.

The Canelo School was just one of a series of small one-room schoolhouses that dotted Santa Cruz County in the early part of the century. The only way to get around was by foot, horse or wagon, and since children could not travel long distances, these small schools sprang up everywhere. The little ranching communities of Rain Valley, Parker Canyon, Lochiel, San Rafael, Sonoita, Vaughn, Empire and Greaterville all had their own schools.

Dances were often held on Saturdays at the schoolhouses. Everyone brought their entire family for an evening of fun. The children danced until they dropped of exhaustion and were put to sleep on the back seat of their parents' car. The dancing went on until all hours. During prohibition, the local men brought their home brew in bottles and hid them outside in the grass hummocks. Everyone walked outside cautiously, so as not to knock over a bottle. The brew was poured into Mason jars for imbibing, and according to Austin Moss, "you could tell the serious drinkers by the ring on their noses. The Mason jar would make a semi-circular mark on the bridge of the drinker's nose that was unmistakable."

In the late 20s or early 30s Stayton Brooks' mother was the teacher and she found it too difficult to navigate the 30-mile drive from Patagonia over bumpy, dirt roads every day. She partitioned off a section of the one-room building as living quarters for herself and her two children. She then was able to live in the school during the week and return to her home and husband on the weekends.

Fern Bartlett Collie, first teacher at the Canelo School, and her sister, Chopeta Bartlett Collie who taught at Rain Valley. The two sisters married two brothers. Circa 1900.
Photo courtesy Marka Moss and Jane Woods.

Byrd Lindsey attended the school from 1941 through 1943. Cora Everhart was his first teacher. He remembers two little girls playing on the grounds and one of them was eating a luscious chocolate chip cookie. All of a sudden, Ole Kid, a horse ridden to school each day by one of the Arrington boys, sneaked up on her and snagged the cookie, gulping it down in no time flat. The little girl, quite incensed, complained bitterly to the teacher. In those days parents did not complain if the teacher punished an errant child. When the culprit's owner talked back to her, the teacher picked him up by his collar and "shook the living daylights out of him," according to Byrd. Ole Kid had already happily ingested the treat and was completely indifferent to the punishment being meted out to his hapless owner.

Byrd got the job of custodian in his final year at the school. He was paid $5 per month to perform his duties, which included arriving early to sweep, build a fire, clean the blackboard and clap the erasers. His mother insisted that he put his princely wages in the Bisbee Bank each month, and when he had amassed enough funds, he spent the proceeds to purchase a milk cow.

The golden age of the Canelo School drew to an end in 1948. The student body had dwindled to a mere three children. Jim Pyeatt was a seventh grader and Pete

Shepherd and his sister were a few years younger. Dorothy Hardy, the teacher, was known as the "Tequila Queen" according to Pyeatt, "because of the bottle she kept handy in her desk drawer," perhaps to ward off distress over the impending loss of her job. Today, the schoolhouse, located 17 miles south of Sonoita on Route 83, looks much as it did in the old days thanks to several coats of paint and lots of elbow grease provided by Byrd Lindsey and his family.

Betty Barr

Judge Richard Harrison keeps abreast of
the news on the porch of his courtroom/
home in Lochiel. Circa 1905.
Photo courtesy Howard Hathaway

Mary Wilson Harrison, the wife of Judge Harrison.
She was the grandmother of Jim Hathaway.
Photo courtesy Hathaway family.

Betty Barr

Judge Richard Harrison

Lochiel

The slumbering community of Lochiel, nestled in the soft curve of rolling hills that dot the border between Arizona and Sonora, gives little hint that in the 1880s it was the bailiwick of a flamboyant frontier judge named Richard Harrison as well as the headquarters of the San Rafael Ranch, a huge cattle empire built by Colin Cameron.

Judge Harrison was installed as the first postmaster of La Noria, as the town was known in those days, on July 24, 1882. Several years later the national boundary was surveyed between Arizona and Sonora and the correct placement of the international border cut the little community in two. The Mexican side of the line continued to be known as La Noria, which in Spanish means a draw well or a well operated with a wheel. Cameron named the American portion Lochiel, perhaps in deference to his Scottish forebearers.

Judge Harrison had come to Lochiel from Virginia by way of California and the Gold Rush of 1849. He had acquired large tracts of land as payment for his surveying services in Ukiah, but a love of horseracing had taken its toll on his land holdings and he traveled to Arizona, settling in Lochiel in the late 1870s. There he served as Justice of the Peace, holding court in his own home and dispensing his own brand of justice.

At one memorable hearing, the defendant in an assault case was Jim Parker, whose daughter was married to Judge Harrison's grandson, Jim Hathaway. Parker had reportedly confronted a man at a roundup and accused him of stealing some cattle. When the argument became heated, Parker bent a branding iron over the alleged thief's head. The Judge didn't have much liking for the plaintiff, but since Parker had admitted the assault, he felt he had to impose some kind of punishment on the guilty party. He ruled in favor of the plaintiff and ordered the defendant to bring to court one jug of mescal. The defendant and the judge then retired to the front porch where they shared the penalty and reminisced about their days in California.

Mescal, derived from the agave plant, was evidently a favorite beverage of the judge. Another occasion involving this potent drink had happened several years previously when Jim Hathaway, the judge's grandson, was living with him. The ten-year-old Jim was quite proud of his little horse and always welcomed an excuse to take him for a ride.

One thirsty afternoon, the judge directed the youngster to mount his horse and ride across the border to the little town of Santa Cruz and bring him back a bottle of the brew. One of the patrons at the saloon was a big, mean-looking, half-drunk man who was cursing gringos and casting covetous eyes on the youngster's horse. The bartender tried to divert the troublemaker while Jim slipped out the back and galloped off with the bottle stowed safely in his saddlebag.

About a mile down the road Jim heard the sound of galloping hoof beats and suddenly the bandito loped past him, lashing Jim's horse with his rope as he went by. Unfazed, the plucky youngster pursued him and whipped out at the bandit's horse, which bucked violently throwing him

Ten-year-old Jim Hathaway was proud of his little horse and welcomed every opportunity to ride him. Circa 1902.
Photo courtesy Hathaway family.

to the ground and knocking him out cold. It was possible his neck was broken, as he never moved a muscle, but the boy was frightened that the man would come to and try to kill him.

Young Jim's prized possession was a fancy knife with a peephole. If you held it up to the light at just the right angle, you could see a lady inside, wearing an old-fashioned bathing suit. The knife was the envy of his classmates and he kept it razor sharp. He pulled out the knife, ran over to his attacker and stabbed at him. He dragged the unconscious man over to a nearby abandoned mine shaft, pushed him in and then jumped back on his horse and raced, hell bent for leather, back to Lochiel. When Judge Harrison finally got his white-faced and terrified grandson to tell him what had happened, he just listened in silence. He made no pronouncement one way or the other, but never again did he send the boy across the line for mescal. No rumblings were heard about a body being found near Santa Cruz. The judge figured the man could have been dazed and was later able to make his way back to town or perhaps the sides of the mine caved in and hid the body.

The judge had four sons: Charlie, Jim, Dick and Harry. Dick died in a battle over stock watering rights in the San Rafael Valley while still in his 20s and Harry was killed at age 34 by a disgruntled drunk customer at a saloon he owned in Washington Camp.

This colorful community, located in San Antonio Canyon on the east slope of the Patagonia Mountains, was the site of many hair-raising activities. A Chinese man known locally as "Old Kang" ran a store there for many years. One day a Mexican came into the store and attempted a holdup. Kang reached down under the counter where his cat was innocently snoozing, grabbed it by the hind leg and slammed the hapless creature into the head of the robber. The would-be burglar not only received a tremendous blow to the side of his head; he was almost clawed to death in the process.

Another robber attempting a holdup at Old Kang's ended up being shot to death. When the bandit's daughter came into the store to complain, Old Kang told her that was what you could expect when you hold up a store. Old Kang out-lived both of his Chinese wives, and when he died he had a Mexican wife and stepson. He had buried all his valuables so his wife wouldn't find them after he was gone, but shortly after his death the house caught fire and looters made off with all his possessions.

Despite Lochiel's remote location, Judge Harrison was a well-known and well-respected member of the bar. Just inside the door of Old Main on the University of

Arizona campus is a marble plaque listing Richard Harrison, Lochiel, Arizona, as a member of the first Board of Regents. Perhaps because of his honored status, the Judge was not easily intimidated. On one occasion he was summoned to appear in Tucson as a witness in a lawsuit. The presiding judge scolded him for arriving at court without a coat and sent him home to dress properly. Harrison did an about face, stalked off to the livery stable, got his horse and rode back to Lochiel. When he returned quite some time later the judge yelled, "Where have you been," whereupon Harrison replied, "You told me to go home and fetch my coat!"

Judge Harrison spent the rest of his life in Lochiel and is buried in the Nogales Cemetery. His sons Dick and Harry were laid to rest in a small family graveyard at Lochiel.

Roundup in the San Rafael Valley early 1900s. From left standing: Dan Sheehy, Frank and Lee Parker. Seated: George and Duke Parker. Reclining: Jess Bland and Dick Harrison. Frank, Jess and Dick all died shortly after photo was taken. Photo courtesy Kathy Goodwin.

Betty Barr

Jim Hathaway, on rearing horse, with cowhand, Tomas Heredia, on the Patagonia Road in 1930.
Both men are buried at Black Oak Cemetery.
Photo courtesy Howard Hathaway

Jim Hathaway

Lawman, rancher, frontiersman

The imposing figure of Jim Hathaway loomed large over Santa Cruz County in the first half of the twentieth century. Lawman, rancher, frontiersman. All these terms and many others have been used to describe Hathaway; but to his son, Howard, this complex and complicated man is remembered with a mixture of awe, respect, admiration, love and yes, a healthy dose of fear.

Awe for the feats of daring and raw courage necessary for survival on the tough Arizona/Sonora border, respect for the stern disciplinarian who required that his children address him as "Father," admiration for the myriad of skills perfected in forging a life on the frontier, love for the father who labored against tremendous odds to ensure college educations for his three children, and fear of the tough lawman who was skilled with the gun and quick to use it.

The key to unlocking the enigma of Hathaway's dual persona most probably lies in his beginnings. Jim was born in the border town of Lochiel in 1892 where his father, Lincoln, taught in the one-room schoolhouse. His mother, Nellie, was the daughter of Lochiel's Judge Richard Harrison and was several years younger than Linc. In fact, she had been a pupil of his at the school before their marriage.

Jim's tough and sometimes cruel side could have had its roots in his early life. His mother, Nell Harrison Hathaway, although known as a fun-loving beauty, had no interest in family life. In later years, Jim confided to his wife that his mother

Customs officer Lincoln Hathaway, Jim's father, in the early 1900s.
Photo courtesy Howard Hathaway.

forced him to walk barefoot through a patch of sand stickers and wouldn't pick him up. He also remembered being left trapped in his highchair for long periods while she went visiting friends.

His father, Lincoln, soon joined the Customs Service in Nogales and was gone from home for weeks at a time patrolling the border. He worried about his children growing up on the rough border and in 1900 he sent Nell and the two boys to his hometown in York, Nebraska, while he remained in Nogales. Life in the flat farm country of the Midwest didn't sit well with Nell and the children, and within a year they were back in Arizona. Linc died of pneumonia when Jim was only 12 years old. Nell remarried and moved to Tucson and the rebellious teenager would pack up his saddlebags and ride out into the mountains west of town where he would camp out alone for days at a time.

Early one evening he was returning from one of these sojourns, riding a burro and leading another with a deer carcass strapped across it. Spying a ranch house, he stopped to see if he could get some water. The rancher noticed the fresh deer and demanded it in payment before he would allow Jim or the animals to drink. The young boy galloped off rather than let the rancher take unfair advantage of him.

Predators also posed problems and when a mountain lion tried to attack his burro in camp Jim shot at it with an old pistol. The pistol backfired somehow and the recoil knocked him out for a few minutes. When he came to he found the mountain lion dead at his feet. Thus was born his knack of surviving in the wilds and protecting himself against two legged as well as four legged adversaries.

Within two years Nell also passed away and the young boy moved back to Santa Cruz County, living first with his Uncle Jim Harrison and then Uncle Dick. Not

Jim Hathaway's fraternal grandparents in the late 1800s. Grandmother Catherine Wheeler Hathaway was a practicing medium. Legend has it that one day Jim scribbled a future date on a shed door. Prophetically, it was the date that his clairvoyant grandmother passed away.
Photo courtesy Marion Hathaway Bittinger.

long afterwards, Uncle Dick was shot by a neighbor in a fight over watering rights in the San Rafael Valley. Uncle Harry ran a saloon in Washington Camp and was shot by a rowdy customer. Both Harrison brothers met their untimely deaths while still in their twenties.

In later years, it was hard for him to adapt to the role of family man. His daughter Marion says that when her father was at home no one spoke at the dinner table because he was usually in a bad mood and would not answer when they asked him questions. Howard adds, "Oftentimes he would take offense at someone and there would be no relenting in his cold anger for years, maybe for all time."

Jim Hathaway was barely out of his teens in 1912, but by then he had been on his own for years and was eager for adventure no matter how wild or reckless. One night he was heading for his brother's place on the Nogales/Washington Camp Road and all his senses were on the alert. He had heard by the grapevine that an Indian outlaw from Sonora had spotted his prized horse and boasted that he could steal it. Suddenly shots rang out from some bushes at the side of the dark roadway. The bandit had underestimated his quarry, however. Within seconds Jim had his new automatic pistol out and was firing in the direction of the shots, and spurring his horse madly at the same time. No one ever knew if the would-be horse thief was hit by bullets, but a story made the rounds that, "An Indian got stung by a bee when he tried to steal Hathaway's horse."

By the time he was twenty years old, Jim was fluent in Spanish and had many friends in Sonora. Political unrest was rampant in Mexico and Jim was right in the thick of many revolutionary gun battles. One group of guerillas he rode with included a man called "Yaqui Quinn." The Mexican captain suspected Yaqui Quinn of being a spy and he started to question him. Quinn's answers made him even more suspicious and the captain pulled his pistol and shot him off his horse. Quinn rolled into a ravine and three others from the troop scrambled down the slope to pilfer his meager possessions. He had a particularly fine pair of boots and one of the men began tugging at them, but the Indian was not quite dead yet and began kicking and jerking. The startled revolutionaries dropped their booty and Yaqui Quinn was left to die in peace with his boots on. No one was brave enough to argue with the ghost of Yaqui Quinn.

Soon afterwards he joined some Mexican friends on a foray to Sonora where warring political factions were engaging in skirmishes on a daily basis. It was guerilla-type warfare, waged on horseback, with each side outfitted with whatever rifles and pistols they could get their hands on. Jim's group had pushed the enemy back from an advantageous position and made camp for the night near a ranch house.

The first part of the evening was spent in a raucous victory celebration, but finally all quieted down for the night. In the early hours just before dawn, Jim awoke with a bad feeling. Everything seemed quiet, but he got up and noiselessly pulled on his boots, saddled his horse and rode quietly out of camp to investigate. He got to a vantage point at the top of a hill and when he turned to look down at the camp he was horrified to see the enemy attacking his friends, yelling and shooting in a mad frenzy. Within minutes the camp was wiped out and Jim was the only one to escape with his life.

Capture and imprisonment in Sonora was a fate to be avoided at all costs. Jim described the prison to his son, Howard. "A favorite torture was to withhold food and drink for three or four days. Then the prisoners were allowed all the tortillas and water they wanted. A generous helping resulted in a doughy mass of rapidly swelling material, which caused death by intestinal stoppage and bloat.

A sheer cliff at one end of the yard served as a backstop for prisoners facing the firing squad, and one of Jim's friends was awaiting his fate there. Jim managed to get the death sentence removed, but the man soon got into a fight with a guard and was re-sentenced to death. He told Jim he didn't regret it, he just couldn't put up with the jerks that ran the place.

About this time, Jim got a job as foreman of a big ranch in Sonora. He hadn't been there for long when a revolutionary band rode into the ranch and captured all the hands, including Jim. They threw a rope over a large tree and began to hang the cowboys, one by one. While they were busy executing one of the hands, Jim managed to grab a gun and escape on horseback. They chased him for miles, but he had his wire-cutters with him, and was able to cut the border fence and make it back to the safety of the U.S. He never told anyone how many he had to kill to make his getaway.

Howard Hathaway tells of a time when he was about twelve years old (around 1928) and came home from school one day to find Jim, lying propped up in bed in the front room, an unprecedented event to say the least. From his earliest days, Howard had been trained to call Jim "Father," although all the other kids addressed their fathers as "Dad" or "Pop." When he said, "Hello, Father," Jim looked at him with no recognition in his eyes.

Jim Hathaway's ranch on River Road between Nogales and Patagonia where Grandma Emma Parker delivered Hathaway's youngest child, Marion, June 22, 1926.
Photo courtesy Marion Hathaway Bittinger.

Howard fled to the kitchen where his mother told him that Jim had been overseeing a fencing project when his horse fell down a steep rocky cliff and he had hit his head. The Mexican laborers had carried him down Palomas Canyon to the house and it was several days before he came to and could recognize his family. Eighteen years later a piece of bone started to poke through his forehead and after he wiggled it out he joked that he must be growing horns!

The Hathaway homestead, where they lived during the early twenties, was located between Patagonia and Nogales. It extended from the Patagonia foothills to the Santa Cruz River. Over a low hill just west of their frame house was a mesquite flat which later became the Nogales Airport.

Jim had two Mexican cowboys working for him named Valentino and Pabolino. When Howard was around six or seven they would take him up the canyon where they were digging a well. Jim and the two workers would take turns being lowered into the hole by windlass to do the digging. When it came time for a dynamite charge, the man in the hole would light the fuse, the other two would draw him up as quickly as possible and then all three would run to safety.

Howard remembered how Pabolino carved him a little man out of the base of a century plant and roasted it over a mesquite fire. While the men were working, he spent happy hours chewing the sweet juice from it.

The other worker, Valentino, was a large, homely, cheerful man. One day he and Jim came in from riding fence and found one of Jim's Spanish-speaking American friends, whom Valentino had never met before, sleeping on the porch. Jim picked up a six-shooter, loaded it with blanks and told Valentino what to do next. Valentino went over to the sleeping guest, shook him awake and shouted, "Despierta! Te voy a matar!" ("Wake up! I'm going to kill you!") The frightened visitor awoke to the sight of a big, ugly desperado shooting three or four blanks at him at close range and Jim Hathaway howling with laughter in the background.

Years later Howard heard that Valentino had turned outlaw in Sonora and had been executed, but others told him that Jim himself may have shot him. Whatever the truth, his compadres made up songs in his honor and for many years mariachis in the border bars would sing requests for "Valentino de la Sierra."

In the early 1930s, Jim started building a place in Parker Canyon. He had purchased three adjoining ranches close to the spot where his wife Virginia's family had homesteaded in the 1850s. One day in 1933 when the house was almost completed, Jim was working inside when he heard the sound of horses approaching in the dry streambed. He slipped into a space under the floor, peeked through a vent and saw three Mexicans stop in front and tie their horses up to the fence. They came up to the house and thinking no one was home, came in and started fixing themselves some lunch.

Jim had a curtain hanging over a small recess near the fireplace where he was planning to install a faucet. One end of an open pipe protruded into the alcove and the other end was in the space where Jim was hiding. He heard one of the cowboys say in Spanish, "Look at that little curtain!" From underneath the floor, Jim had been blowing through the pipe and making the curtain flutter. Jim listened to the footsteps as one of the men cautiously approached the mysteriously fluttering curtain. When he figured the man was reaching for the drape, he roared through the pipe.

The three intruders reached the door at the same time and became wedged in their frantic attempt to escape. The front steps weren't in yet and the door was three feet off the ground. After a brief struggle, the three broke loose, tumbled out the door and charged towards their horses. They made such a racket that the horses spooked and bolted off down the canyon with the intruders in hot pursuit on foot. Jim took great delight when the news spread that he was building a "haunted house."

The house Jim built for the family now lies at the bottom of Parker Canyon Lake.

Betty Barr

Virginia Parker, at age 18, shortly before
her elopement with Jim Hathaway. Circa
1913.
Photo courtesy Hathaway family.

Virginia Parker Hathaway

Parker Canyon

Sweet and even-tempered Virginia Parker was born in 1895, the eleventh of twelve children of Jim and Emma Parker, and named after her future husband's aunt, Virginia Harrison. Virginia wasn't born at the Parker homestead (now under water at Parker Canyon Lake) but at what was then called the Scotia place. Her parents were living there while her dad was logging and hauling pine logs by oxen to the nearby settlement at Sunnyside.

Son Howard recounts this story in his memoirs: "One day when Virginia (Virge) was about 17, she accosted the horseman who delivered the mail on the Parker Canyon/Lochiel route and jokingly told him that she sure would like him to bring her a letter next time around. The ever-helpful mailman told Jim Hathaway that Virge Parker wanted to receive a letter, and he wrote to her right away." Jim was one of the Harrison/Hathaway clan from the border town of Lochiel, known across the county as hard-nosed rugged individualists.

Howard's memoir continues, "Thus began the courtship. Jim knew her brothers, George, Duke and Frank, who had ranches in the San Rafael Valley, and pretty soon he was invited to supper at the Parker's where he was thoroughly intimidated by her father, Jim Parker.

"Virge told him he would have to ask her Pa for her hand and so he got up his nerve one evening as the two men were sitting on the front porch after dinner discussing cattle prices. Virge was strategically placed at a listening post just inside

Jim and Emma Parker, Virginia Hathaway's parents, at the homestead in Parker Canyon. Circa 1918.
Photo courtesy Howard Hathaway and Marion Hathaway Bittinger.

the door and heard Jim ask, 'Is it all right if Virginia and I get married?' Grandpa said, "Whit?" (His pronunciation of what). Jim offhandedly repeated his question and Grandpa said, "I guess so," and they returned to discussing cattle.

"Armed with this rather nebulous permission, the young couple planned their elopement with enthusiasm. Jim announced that he would pick her up in a horse-drawn buggy at a certain time and day and if she didn't come then, he wouldn't return for her. On the agreed upon day, Virge hurried through all her chores, prompting her mother to scold her that everything didn't have to get done in one day, but she kept the secret to herself.

"When she heard the buggy approaching she retrieved her hidden suitcase and rushed outside to the surprise of her parents who finally realized that their daughter was eloping. Jim urged the horse to a trot, Virge shouted her good-byes, and her astonished parents stood in the yard with tears in their eyes watching their daughter leave home.

"They reached Nogales and were waiting to catch the train when they were spotted by Judge Duffy, the husband of one of Virge's sisters. When he learned what his eighteen-year-old sister-in-law was planning, he hurried home to fetch his wife so they could put a stop to the foolishness.

"The train arrived before he and Annie (Parker Duffy) returned, and the young couple made it to Tucson. They arrived too late to get a license so Jim got Virge a room at the hotel, but Jim's old friend and former employer, Sheriff Forbes, saved the day by arranging for a late afternoon wedding. A proud and happy Jim returned to the hotel, crossed out "Miss Virginia Parker" and proudly signed in as Mr. and Mrs. Jim Hathaway."

And so Virginia began a life of hardship and adventure with Jim Hathaway that was not to end until her untimely death in 1951. For a short time they lived in Gila Bend where Jim ran the general store. They soon moved to Uncle Dick Harrison's place in the Patagonias and Jim built the stone house where they lived from 1915 to 1918. Uncle Dick had died at age 24 in a battle over stock watering rights in the San Rafael Valley.

Pancho Villa was leading raids across the border at this time and General Pershing had been sent to quell the riots but met with little success. One day a band of Mexicans rode into Patagonia and the ranchers joined together to ward them off. Virge galloped to a nearby ranch that had a phone and called for troops at Camp Little (in Nogales) to come help. When the soldiers finally arrived, the officer in charge looked over the situation and called back to camp reporting it as a false alarm. The usually timid Virge exploded in anger and called him a coward, shaming him into leading his men to the battle where the Mexicans were beaten back across the line.

Howard remembered that among the first words he learned to say were, "Listen, (pause) it's nothing," mimicking his parents as they strained for sounds of raiders. One night Virge was hiding in the corral when Jim rode in and started unsaddling. She made a noise to scare him and he nearly shot her with his six-shooter. She would often recount the story with great hilarity, but her husband never did find it amusing.

In a letter written to the author shortly before his death in November 2000, Howard commented on his strict upbringing, "I never had a date or went to a dance or party in high school. How my college classmates razzed me. Suddenly, my par-

Virginia and Jim Hathaway posed for a formal portrait with their two oldest children, Howard and Helen. Circa 1924. Photo courtesy Hathaway family.

ents were urging me to get married. A 180-degree shift, like training a vine to grow a certain way, then when its trunk is well-developed, trying to make it grow in the opposite direction. As Lil' Abner of the old comic strip would say, 'Cornfoozin' but not amoozin.'"

After Howard was born in 1916, the family moved to the Patagonia homestead. Jim gathered mesquite and scrub oak for firewood and hauled it home with his wagon and team. Virge cooked on a wood-burning stove and hauled water to the house in buckets. Howard recalled when his little sister, Helen, was born his mother would tell him to watch the sleeping baby while she ran a quarter of a mile up the wash to fetch a bucket of water.

At the age of five, Howard started at the Santa Cruz River School (called Little Red today). The one-room schoolhouse had eight grades and two teachers. He rode his little filly, Mary Lee, down Palomas wash to the county road and on to school. He had to go through a wire gate on the way and his dad had set a mounting block there so the five-year-old could get back on board after closing the gate.

Mary Lee came in handy when impromptu horse races were held. A youngster bareback was a lot lighter and faster than an adult with a heavy stock saddle. Jim would anchor Howard to the filly with a long felt strap so he wouldn't bounce off and the race was on! Money was in short supply, so bets could be a saddle, spurs, a calf - whatever was valuable. Virge was not amused when Jim lost all her chickens on one such wager.

Taquachee, an old Mexican who lived on the Santa Cruz, was a tall mustachioed gentleman who stuffed his pants legs down into old-fashioned, high-topped boots. One day Jim met Taquachee on the trail and as they sized up each other's mounts, they decided to race, winner take the other's horse. When Jim lost he told the winner to ride home with him and he would unsaddle and give him the horse. Taquachee announced that Jim was sitting on his mare and Jim ended up walking home, packing his saddle. Taquachee renamed the mare, "La Captiva" and she became his prized possession.

When Jim won the next race and went to the loser's house to collect the chickens that had been wagered, Taquachee told him to catch his chickens himself. They were not penned up and as Jim started chasing them, Taquachee yelled to his kids, "Scatter those chickens, don't let him catch them." Jim ended up with two or three chickens out of a flock of 20 or more.

In 1926 Grandma Emma Parker delivered the baby of the family, Marion, at the River Road ranch near Nogales where the family lived at that time. Marion says, "Howard was my idol. He was ten years older and in my eyes could do no wrong. Tiya (Helen) was the only girl until I came along and was my dad's favorite. She was at an awkward age, thin with straight hair and I was cute, chubby and had curls. That all changed as I got older, she said in an aside. Mama made Helen fix my hair and I dreaded it. She pulled my hair and hit me with the brush."

Marion continues, "He (Howard) could never satisfy my dad. He was criticized morning, noon and night. By the time I came along, I think Papa had softened somewhat. I used to climb in bed with him and he would tell me stories. I spilled my milk one time and he spanked me. It was the only time he ever hit me. He felt terrible. The next day he brought me a doll. I named it Spanky."

Jim's Mexican friends got him appointed a colonel in the rebel army during the political unrest in the late 1920s and issued him an ornate uniform with epaulets and a sword. He would never wear the costume and it hung in the closet for many years. Marion remembers that, "He was a rebel and wouldn't conform to social ways. He fought in the Mexican Revolution just because he wanted to. Mother wore a little leather pouch around her neck that was filled with money and instructions that if he didn't come home she was to get on a horse

Jim and Virginia Hathaway's three children, Howard, Marion and Helen. Circa 1927. Photo courtesy Marion Hathaway Bittinger.

and ride to Nogales as fast as she could." Virge and the children were forbidden to cross the border for fear that they would be kidnapped and held for ransom.

The family was living temporarily at a little adobe house near the Santa Cruz School while Jim tried unsuccessfully to remove a squatter from a house on his ranch. The squatter was determined to stay and even hired a couple of Mexican renegades to harass the Hathaways. Virginia was home alone one day when one of them showed up, destroyed some of her things and casually strolled away. A few nights later the children were asleep in the bedroom and Jim, Virge and Valentino, their hand, were in the kitchen roasting chilis.

The men stepped outside for water and one of the outlaws fired at them. Valentino shot back and the man rolled over and played possum. When Valentino walked over to him, the man jumped up and ran for the kitchen screen door where Virge was frozen in fear. The outlaw had his mouth wide open, yelling at her when Jim took aim. The bullet went in one cheek and out the other without breaking a tooth. By that time, neighbors joined in to help and the sheriff arrived and took the family to Nogales to spend the rest of the night with relatives.

In 1951 Virginia's life turned upside down. Life had gotten easier. All the children were grown and married and she and Jim were living on their ranch in the Huachucas. During a gathering for a livestock sale, Jim and a neighbor, Juan Telles, got into an argument that escalated throughout the day and culminated with a shootout at the stockyards in Sonoita. Telles was killed and Jim was arrested and tried in Nogales for second-degree murder.

Although he was cleared of the charges, the Hathaway family's happiness and relief at the "Not Guilty" verdict was soon dashed by the shock of a completely unexpected and tragic occurrence. A short two months later, daughter Helen's husband, Wally Wilson, arrived at the ranch with a load of hay he had hauled down from Chandler. He didn't see anyone around, so he unloaded the hay and then went up to the house where he found Virginia lying on the living room floor, dead of a heart attack. She was 56 years old.

Howard mourned, "There were causes aplenty to result in her dying before her time. Years and years of living with this mate of hers, whose moods were myriad and who lived through one death-defying adventure after another, would have been sufficient to cause the demise or the departure of most women. Jim himself had remarked that no one else could have stayed with him so long. Many were those who admired Jim for his bravery and daring feats. (Few failed) to take note of Virge's sterling qualities and her unobtrusive presence in the background."

Jim Hathaway served as deputy sheriff in Nogales for eight years, from 1925 to 1933.
Photo courtesy Howard Hathaway and Marion Hathaway Bittinger.

Jim Hathaway

Manhunter

The sleepy towns of Ambos Nogales served as an escape route into Mexico for many notorious criminals facing charges in the United States in the 1920s and 30s. With Jim Hathaway's extensive network of friends and informants on both sides of the line, he soon became known as the number one "go to" person when a wanted man "went south."

Howard Hathaway remembers that his father "cracked some important cases and nailed some notorious criminals. He made a number of lasting enemies during his years as a lawman. Some of these thirsted for revenge long after he was no longer a deputy. He didn't fall victim to any because of his own wariness, whetted to a fine edge by a lifetime of constant danger."

One of the most notorious cases during his eight years as constable in Nogales was the Mother Modie incident. On October 19, 1925, the townsfolk of Nogales were horrified to learn of a terrible crime committed against one of their most beloved citizens. Gertrude "Mother" Modie ran a lodging house in town. She was known as a soft touch because she would never turn anyone away from her door if they needed a place to stay. She was well-known and loved by every rancher, prospector, homesteader and cowboy on both sides of the border.

Constable Jim Hathaway got the call early in the morning and hurried to the rooming house where he found Mother Modie lying in a pool of blood, dangerously near death. The 72-year-old woman had been beaten and slashed with a knife. The odor of charred flesh in the room led to the grisly discovery that her hands and feet had been brutally burned. The blood-splattered bedroom had been thoroughly ransacked and Jim immediately knew her attacker must have been a stranger, because everyone in northern Sonora and southern Arizona knew Mother Modie had been penniless for a long time. She did have many items of jewelry and gold nuggets, however, given to her by grateful people she had helped over the years. These few treasures were missing. The doctor pronounced that there was not much hope of recovery for the battered woman and Hathaway was incensed. He vowed he would leave no stone unturned in his search for the perpetrator of such an evil act.

There were few clues to be had. Jim checked the pawnshops and railroads and questioned suspects to no avail. He decided to take a second look at the crime scene and discovered that the ceiling light bulb was bloody. Further inspection revealed that the wall switch was defective and the attacker had stood on a chair to unscrew the bulb, leaving a good set of prints. (Jim sent the prints to the FBI and a return wire confirmed a match to Carlos Silvas, an escapee from Leavenworth, and included a picture and his description as a Mexican and Mission Indian from California, who had served time for smuggling Chinese and Mexican women into the U.S.)

Knowing that the wanted man had probably left town, Jim decided to "go across the street" into Mexico. Hathaway had absolutely no authority in the Sister City, and if he did apprehend the criminal there, would have had no legal recourse to return him to justice in the U.S. However, Jim's methods of dealing with situations such as this were unorthodox and this detail had little or no bearing on his course of action.

Jim contacted Colonel Enrique Velasquez, commandant of the local fort and an old compadre from his Mexican army days, and assured him that he was in Sonora unofficially, was unarmed, and would report any findings about the case to the local police. He was totally bi-lingual and could think in either Spanish or English and Nogales, Sonora, was as familiar to him as his own backyard. In spite of his promise to Velasquez, when Jim spotted a huge unkempt man trying to sell jewelry in a local store he followed him.

The man, who closely matched the description of Silvas, slipped into a local bar. Jim knew of a door leading to an alley so he bypassed the main entrance, hurried to the alley and caught Silvas darting out the back. He tackled him and had just about secured him when a crowd formed and started chanting and calling for the release of someone they assumed was a Mexican citizen. A struggle ensued and Silvas reached behind his neck and pulled a 12-inch stiletto from under his collar. He crouched menacingly, threatening Hathaway with the knife. Within seconds a stunned Silvas was lying on his back in the middle of the street with his knife 20 feet away. Somehow Jim got to the knife first and held it to the suspect's back, jabbing him every time the crowd got too close for comfort. He slapped one handcuff on Silvas and the other on his own wrist.

The crowd grew to a mob, yelling for the blood of the gringo. A rock-thrower on a nearby rooftop managed to knock off Hathaway's hat, a favorite that had cost him $100. He scrambled to retrieve it and jammed it back on his bloody head before finding a fresh spot on Silvas' back to prick with the stiletto. Two hours went by and Jim was just about out of energy when Colonel Velasquez was finally able to break through the crowd and come to his rescue.

The colonel was distraught to find that Jim had reneged on his promise to turn his findings over to Mexican police, and instead, had apprehended the criminal himself on Mexican soil. He said, "Compadre, you have caused much trouble and for what? This man is a Mexican and you know he cannot be extradited. Not even the president of Mexico could send Carlos Silvas out of this country."

But Jim had another ace up his sleeve. Unlocking the cuffs, he turned the prisoner over to Velasquez to be locked up in the military prison while he hurried back to the U.S. The following morning he arrived at the border and presented a communiqué from the FBI showing that when Silvas was arrested for the first time he had listed his nationality as American Indian. Acting on this information, the Mexican authorities turned Silvas over to Jim as an alien criminal illegally in Mexico. Colonel Velasquez provided military escort as Hathaway and his prisoner made their historic trek to International Avenue pelted by bricks, stones, bottles and vegetables from the furious mob.

Rumor on the Arizona side had it that Mother Modie had died, and Americans gathered at the border hoping to assault the suspect as he crossed over. Seeing them, Silvas balked, but Velasquez facilitated his crossing with a timely placed saber prick on his backside. Mother Modie recovered enough to appear in court in her wheelchair and identify Silvas as the man who had robbed and tortured her. He was sentenced to life at the Arizona State Prison in Florence.

Howard often remarked that much of his information about Jim's cases came from other sources. "My dad wouldn't say much at home, so Mom and we kids

Capt. R. Havelock-Bailie wrote magazine articles about the exploits of Jim Hathaway, that appeared in Startling Detective Adventures, Apr. 1939 and Vital Detective Cases, Apr. 1946. Barr photo.

knew little of what was going on. What events I found out about were mainly gleaned by overhearing conversations between him and his friends, Mexicans and Americans." Most of Howard's information about the Mother Modie case came from a magazine article by Capt. R. Havelock-Bailie in 'Startling Detective Adventures,' April 1939. It was written in the flowery, romantic style of the day and as Jim's longtime friend, Bourn Hayne, said, "Jim didn't always think or act exactly as portrayed," but it did provide a graphic description of one of the important cases he solved during his tenure as Constable.

Many stories of his famous captures depicted him as a two-gun, pistol packing man-hunter who had seen service in a four-year career as a colonel in the Mexican army. This was not really accurate, according to son Howard. "I never saw him with anything except a .38 in a right-hand holster and in later years he had a .357 Magnum. He did have commissions at various times (in the Mexican army) and was involved in several battles and campaigns, but not in a prolonged or full-time capacity," Howard wrote in his memoirs.

In 1929 a nasty revolution was being waged in Mexico between the loyalist forces of the newly installed president, General Plutarco Elias Calles, and the revolutionary forces backed by the overthrown president, Aldolfo de la Huerta. Calles reportedly offered Hathaway a reward of 150,000 pesos to apprehend General Alphonso de la Huerta (Adolfo's brother) and turn him over to the military authorities in Sonora.

The general was operating on the American side, furnishing guns and ammunition to the Yaquis, who then delivered them across the border to the revolutionary forces. According to an article by Capt. R. Havelock-Bailie in the April 1939 issue of Startling Detective Adventures, "Within a week after Calles' offer, a car containing de la Huerta and his aide, General Medina, driven by a tall American, crossed the border at a nearly impassable spot. Almost immediately the car was intercepted by federal troops. De la Huerta and Medina were soon before a firing squad. The American was released. Further bloodshed was halted."

A scathing and vastly different account of this same event appeared several years later in the Sunday magazine of a Mexican newspaper, portraying Hathaway as a, "soldier of fortune and a policeman without scruples...Flaunting a complete lack of law enforcement honesty and in violation of American and Mexican laws, sheriff Jim Hathaway...resorted to black subterfuge and delivered (de la Huerta) to military authorities of Sonora so that hours later he should be assassinated together with General Medina, who was also a victim of the evil tricks of the Yankee officer."

A Mexican friend had sent a copy of this Spanish language newspaper to Hathaway. It included a photo with the caption (as translated), "Grim sheriff Jim Hathaway who, for 150,000 pesos, sent to the executioner, General de la Huerta." The photo was of another man entirely and the friend added a handwritten notation under the picture, "This is not Jim. Who is it?" Jim joked that he should sue the paper for printing the wrong photo.

The leader of the forces that installed Calles as president was General Alvaro Obregon. Howard remembered, "Jim pointed out Obregon to Mama and us kids once in Nogales. He was a big, one-armed man. Jim had a horse with the end of one ear off and he named him Obregon."

Jim Hathaway rode horseback across the mountains into Mexico in pursuit of outlaws, ignoring the rules of engagement that govern international boundaries, to bring numerous criminals to justice.
Photo courtesy Hathaway family.

When Jim returned to his ranch after this capture, he found that five of his best horses had been stolen. Following their trail into Mexico he soon discovered that a man named Jose Rodriquez was the guilty party. He sent a note to Rodriquez saying, "Jose, your brother Juan is staying at my house. He will be here when you get back with my horses." About eight days later Rodriquez, looking pale and scared, rode into the ranch herding the five missing horses into the corral and was reunited with his brother.

Havelock-Bailie also recounted other capture stories including the George Gerald incident and the capture of Arnold Bass, a cashier of a bank in King county California. The bank closed its doors after Bass absconded with the funds and a worldwide search was mounted for him. Authorities lost his trail after he disappeared into Mexico but Hathaway located him in Guaymas where he had invested wisely and could not be extradited. Hathaway knew Bass was bored with life there and notices of a fiesta in Nogales were soon prominently displayed in places Bass frequented. Bass took the bait and boarded a train to Nogales with Hathaway right behind him.

Hathaway's agenda was to entice Bass to leave the train before it reached Nogales and somehow get him across the border without raising his suspicions. According to the article, "A hundred miles from Nogales, Hathaway rose from his seat and weaved through the train...then sat down at Bass' side. He whispered, 'They're waiting to pick you up in Nogales,' but Bass refused to speak to him." Then Hathaway inferred that he was an envoy of Bass' wife, sent to warn him of the danger. He told Bass that his wife wanted him to leave the train with Hathaway before it reached Nogales, and she would be waiting at a nearby rendezvous spot.

Bass finally agreed to this plan and jumped off the slow-moving train a few miles before the border town. He became suspicious as they traveled on foot across country and began quizzing Hathaway. He finally balked, saying, "I don't think you're taking me to my wife," whereupon Hathaway, knowing that they had now crossed into American soil, slapped the handcuffs on him. Bass was sentenced to five years in Folsom in January 1936 and Jim received a substantial reward.

The same author tells of another incident when Hathaway went into Mexico looking for a dead man and found a gravesite that had eluded dozens of officers and the Mexican army. In 1929, the rider-less horse of George Gerald, a wealthy cattle rancher and mine owner, had shown up at his Mexican ranch. After extensive searches turned up no trace of him or his body, his relatives appealed to Jim Hathaway for help. Hathaway rented a local horse and headed for the mountains searching for signs of buzzards or coyotes that would lead him to Gerald if he were dead.

Realizing that he was being followed, he backtracked and found three men behind him. Hathaway followed them as they rode into a deep wash, seemed to check on something and then rode away. "Hathaway rode into the wash half an hour later and with little trouble located the body...he had been shot, robbed, thrown into the wash and his body covered with rocks."

After Gerald's body was safely en-route to the U.S., Hathaway attended to his unfinished business with the men who had been following him. He tracked them down with little effort and turned them over to the Mexican authorities.

Jim lived in a constant state of alert because of the many death threats against him from the friends and relatives of people that he had sent to justice over the years. One of the people that he had apprehended for dealing in stolen goods escaped prison, but the court costs and public notoriety that he endured incited his bitter hatred of Hathaway. In 1931 he hired a part-time drifter to kill him.

About this time, a young man had been sent west by his family to experience ranch life and was living with Hathaway at his mountain place in the Huachucas.

One day the hired killer drove up in a touring car with the bad-weather curtains buttoned up. Howard says, "Jim was suspicious because it was a clear day, and after the car stopped, the driver didn't get out." The young visitor was getting lonesome out in the middle of nowhere and went running out to the car to greet the driver before Jim could stop him. The driver had been expecting Jim to come out of the house, but with his plan for a quick shot foiled, decided to accept the invitation to come inside.

There he met Hathaway who had his pistol hidden, but easily acces-

The mountain house that Jim built in the Huachucas is now under water at Parker Canyon Lake. From left: Virginia, Jim, Helen, Marion and Howard in 1936.
Photo courtesy Hathaway family.

sible. After the eastern dude served the stranger coffee, stew and biscuits, Jim sent him out of the room and confronted the stranger. "The caller broke down and confessed that Jim's suspicions were correct....he never came back," Howard relates.

Although this attempt at retribution failed, the man he had arrested did not give up. Several months later a Mexican stranger showed up at the ranch, claiming that his car had broken down. Jim agreed to help him, but was suspicious and became even more so as the man appeared nervous and started whistling. Pretty soon Jim heard an answering whistle up the canyon and the man tried to make a break for it. According to Howard's memoirs, "Jim shot him dead on the spot." Then Jim whistled as if he were the partner and the ambusher whistled back, but kept retreating. "Suddenly Jim saw him stick his head out from behind a tree....got off a quick shot and hit him between the eyes."

When Jim examined the bodies the next day he realized that one of the men was an outlaw wanted for the killing of a Border Patrol officer several years before. "He had the .30-30 which he had used to shoot the officer. A rectangle and cross were carved on the stock to represent a grave."

Howard remembered that a few weeks later two woodcutters came across the remains of one of the bandits and were so spooked that they unhitched their team, mounted the horses and galloped wildly to Canelo, harness trappings flying behind them. He thinks his dad kept the skull of the other bandit because, "there was a skull in the window at the place in the Huachucas for a time. Mexican cowhands were in awe of it and Jim would tease and scare them with it.

Jim Hathaway in late 1951 or early 1952. After the trial
and his wife's subsequent death, Jim moved back to the
mountain cabin in the Huachucas.
Photo courtesy Hathaway family.

Jim Hathaway

Sonoita Shootout

What began as a routine shipping day at Jim Hathaway's cattle ranch in the Huachucas, had, by mid-day, evolved into something that was anything but routine. At 2:30 in the afternoon, Feb.16, 1951, at the stockyards in Sonoita, a gun battle reminiscent of the Wyatt Earp-days of western lore, ended with one man shot to death and another charged with second-degree murder.

Headlines on the front page of the *Nogales Herald*, an evening daily, screamed the news, "Rancher Dies After Gun Fight, Juan Telles Succumbs...Manslaughter Charges Filed Against Well-Known Cattleman."

Newspapers around the state had a heyday with what soon became known as a "Duel in the Sun." The Feb. 25 issue of *The Arizona Republic* reported on the preliminary hearing:

"Jim Hathaway, 59, of Canille (former name of Canelo), wealthy Santa Cruz County cattleman, was bound over to superior court Saturday on a second degree murder charge...Hathaway, taking the stand in his own defense Saturday, told the court the shooting of Telles near the Sonoita stockyards the afternoon of Feb. 16 followed an argument over a woman guest at Hathaway's Canille home. The witness said Telles made insulting and overbearing remarks...at the corrals and repeated the remarks when he met Hathaway at the Sonoita stockyards that afternoon. Hathaway testified he told Telles to stop such comments and added: 'I wouldn't go to your home and cuss out a woman guest you had.' Telles continued with his remarks, Hathaway testified. 'I hit him,' the witness continued, 'and he said, 'You dirty, _____! You just wait here and I'll get my gun and kill you.' Hathaway said he shot Telles when the latter came back and started shooting at him."

Following the preliminary hearing, County Attorney Ruffo Espinosa filed manslaughter charges against Hathaway who was freed on $5,000 bail. Trial date was set to begin at the Nogales Courthouse, May 15, 1951, in front of Judge J. Mercer Johnson, Pima County Superior Court Judge.

Early the morning of the shooting, Hathaway and a few friends had his cattle penned up in his corrals waiting for the Calhoun trucks to arrive and transport them to the Sonoita stockyards. Juan Telles, another local rancher, was to take the excess cattle in his small truck. Jim and Juan were about the same age, had known each other for years and, up to that time, were on friendly terms.

Helping in the corral were Les Guthrie, Cleston Chandler, Bennett Miller and Mrs. Edith Whiteside, all on horseback. They noticed Telles driving in at the wrong entrance and Jim rode over and spoke to him. Telles began laughing and making crude remarks about Jim's wife, Virginia, and Mrs. Whiteside. Hathaway's temper flared, angry words flew back and forth, and Jim kicked Telles off the property.

After the cattle were loaded, Jim, Virginia and Mrs. Whiteside drove to Sonoita in his Dodge pickup. When they arrived, Cicero Martin, the livestock inspector, invited the women to go up to his house for coffee. While they were gone, Telles drove up with a truckload of Frank Harrison's calves. He parked near the weighing scales where Jim and Cleston Chandler were sitting in the pickup. Within minutes, Hathaway and Telles were arguing again, and this time the verbal insults escalated into a pushing and shoving match that culminated with Hathaway slapping Telles several times. Infuriated, Telles rushed back to his truck shouting that he was going home to get his gun and would be back to kill Jim.

Some time passed, the ladies returned from their coffee break, and all seemed calm. Suddenly someone spotted Telles coming back to the stockyards, this time in his Plymouth coupe, armed with a rifle and a six-shooter. Jim ran to his truck, grabbed his 30-30 from behind the seat and ran out into the open, away from the bystanders. Telles took up a position behind his car and fired. Jim dropped to one knee and fired back. Telles pulled out the pistol and fired again. Jim shot through Telles' windshield to try and flush him into the open and Telles ran behind the cattle pen fence. The fence was made of planks about a foot apart and Telles braced his pistol between the planks to steady his shot, but the pistol misfired. At that point Hathaway fired for the third time and knocked Telles down with a bullet to his chest.

The wounded man was loaded into Emory Stoddard's car and rushed to the hospital in Nogales where Dr. Delmar Mock and Dr. Z. B. Noon attended to his injuries. A chartered plane carrying a potentially life-saving blood shipment from Tucson arrived too late to save Telles' life. The *Nogales Herald* noted that Telles had observed his 64th birthday two days before the shooting. He was born in Bisbee and owned and operated an ice and feed store in Tombstone in 1945. He had lived in the Elgin area for 30 years and was survived by his wife Juanita Hughes, three sons and six daughters.

Meanwhile racial tensions were at a fever pitch in the community, which boasted a large Hispanic population. Virginia Hathaway told her children that she had wanted to speak to Mrs.Telles at the preliminary hearing but the attorney advised against it. Several days later she parked in front of Escalada's wholesale grocery store near the international fence. Some kids on the Sonora hillside pelted her car with rocks until Joe Escalada called the nearby Mexican customs officers to stop them. Many of the Hispanic residents of the county stopped attending gatherings and dances at Sonoita and Elgin. Then word made the rounds that a hired killer from Sonora was out to get Jim Hathaway.

One month before the trial was to begin, James E. McDonald, Nogales Police Chief, wrote a letter to Carson Morrow, Chief Customs Officer, Tucson Division. The hand-written letter was delivered by courier pouch and dated April 23, 1951. It read as follows:

> Carson Morrow
> Dear friend:
> I received from a good source that one Anselmo Tadeo & Nacho Barron have been offered $1,500 to bump off Jim Hathaway. They are dickering for more money.
> They are now in Cumaral Son. at this time. Will let you know anything new I learn.
> (Signed) James E. McDonald, Chief of Police

A few weeks later Jim received another hand-written note, this time from his good friend Frank Edgell. It was postmarked May 12, 1951, from Amado, Arizona. Edgell had been trying to discover if the death threat was serious and the letter said in part, "We can't find out a thing about those Sonora men. George has been working pretty hard on it. The Telles(es) don't even know those men. George says that all you have to look out for is that brother who works for Houston.....Frank and Johnnie are getting some information from Romolo Alegria.....When you are up this way....we will go see George and he will tell you....but I think it is all a pack of damn lies. Well Jim this is all for now, but if we find anything bad we will go to your ranch right quick and tell you. (Signed) Your Best Friend, Frank Edgell

The defense called Cicero Martin to the stand. His testimony was described in the *Arizona Daily Star*, May 17 edition.

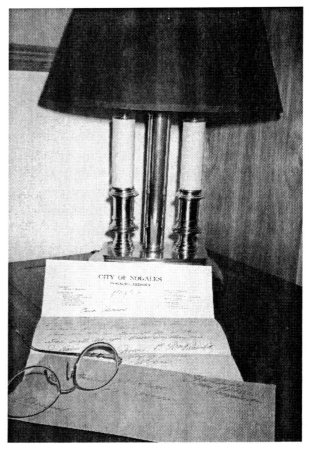

Letter from Nogales Police Chief, James McDonald to Chief Customs Officer Carson Morrow, Tucson District Office, dated Apr. 23, 1951. Envelope indicates the missive traveled via courier to Tucson.
Barr photo.

"Martin, who said he had known Telles and Hathaway since they were in their teens, testified that he saw Telles drive up to the Sonoita stock pens... Prosecution witnesses had related earlier that Telles and Hathaway had engaged in an argument there and that Telles had gone home to get his gun. "Juan threw open the door of his car and jumped out," Martin testified, "I saw a rifle in his hand. He reached around and got a six-shooter off the seat and dropped it on the ground. I looked around and saw Jim had a gun in his left hand and had his right hand up. "Don't shoot, Juan," Jim yelled. Then Juan shot, and Jim shot. They (the shots) were right close together! Juan stooped over and picked up his six-shooter and shot. Then he went around behind his car. The second shot from Jim Hathaway went through the windshield. Juan ran from behind the car toward the stock pen fence and yelled, 'I'll get you yet.' His last shot was through a crack in the fence. Then Jim Hathaway knocked him down."

Frank Harrison was called to the stand and testified, "Telles walked up to Hathaway, cursed him, and made insulting remarks about Mrs. Hathaway and a woman friend. Hathaway slapped Telles twice, knocking his hat off." "I'll go home and get my gun and come back and kill you. Will you wait here?" Harrison quoted Telles as saying. 'I've got those cattle to load and I'll be here until then. I don't want any trouble with you,' Harrison said Hathaway replied. Juan got in his truck still hollering and cussing, and drove off," according to Harrison.

E. A. Stoddard of Sonoita was the first prosecution witness on the opening day of the trial. He testified that Hathaway walked up to Telles who was lying on the ground and said, "I'm sorry it had to happen, Juan." Stoddard said that Telles whispered his reply, "And just over a little joke."

Howard Hathaway came for his father's trial from Oregon, where he was practicing as a veterinarian. His dad told him that if he'd been younger he would have been looking for a fight, but this was one battle he hadn't wanted. "His usual air of confidence was absent and he seemed concerned that he might be found guilty by the jury," Howard recalled.

"During a recess at the trial, I heard Sheriff Lowe tell Dad he would be justified in protecting himself if anyone tried to get him as a result of the gunfight. He was ready for any eventuality and one of the first things he asked me when I arrived was, 'Did you bring a pistol?' Although that mysterious grin accompanied his question, he wasn't joking. He saw to it that I had a gun right away."

Hathaway wasn't the only one who worried about the threat of retribution. A letter dated May 28, 1951, from an old friend, who had moved to Illinois and was serving as pastor of the Sauganash Community Church, ended with this warning: "I know you can take care of yourself, but I can't help sending this little advice – watch out when you are anywhere someone might try to "dry-gulch" you, as we say out in Montana." (Signed) Cyril Richard.

Letters of support and offers of assistance poured in from across the country and the continent. Arizona Congressman Raymond Earhart wrote, "I see by the paper that you had a little trouble. If I can do anything for you in any way...character witness or anything else"...Another, from Ed Charles of Los Altos, California, read, "Jim...we are very anxious to help and I don't mean small sums either...often a good detective agency can be of assistance. We are in good (financial) shape right now...I can have $25,000 there overnight." And a rancher in Chile who signed his name Raphael L. wrote inviting Jim and his family to visit his hacienda for rest and relaxation after the trial.

J. O. (Oscar) Rankin perhaps expressed it best. In a letter mailed from Wickenburg on Apr. 5, he offered, "If there is any way I can help you all, just let me know and I'll be there, Johnny on the spot. I haven't got much of a way to get down there, only an old Jack mule, but if I'm needed it will take me only two days...When you get all straightened out you had better come up and ride awhile with me and we will have some fun...we are getting so old maybe we are kind of feeble minded, but we can still produce more than these dudes. I know damn well I can. Since I saw you last I've been married twice and got three kids...The flies use my head for a skating rink and I have false teeth besides... I'd like to take a few more rides on our old stomping grounds where we used to ride when we were kids."

Rankin's most recent wife added a hand-written postscript to Virginia: "For the past seven years since I have been 'in the family,' I guess I have heard more about 'Old Jim Hathaway' than about any other man. Oscar's fondest memories and deepest affections go back to the years when he and Jim as boys were the terror of the border country and wrecked (sic) their vengeance on anyone who dared to oppose them...Oscar is very proud to call Jim his friend...The feeling he has for you all is only too rare in these modern times but it is none the less sincere." (Signed) Wanda Rankin

Local attorney Duane Bird, Sr., assisted by his teammates Thomas Hall and James V. Robbins, was hired to defend Hathaway on the charge of second-degree murder. Santa Cruz County Attorney, Ruffo Espinosa, prosecuted the case, presided over by Judge J. Mercer Johnson of Pima County Superior Court.

During the proceedings at the Nogales Courthouse, Hathaway, dressed in levis, white shirt and high-heeled cowboy boots, sat quietly at the defense table. On the third day of the trial, the soft-spoken Hathaway took the stand in his own defense. According to the May 18, 1951 edition of the *Nogales International:*

The defendant himself was on the stand from 2:25 to 4:15 yesterday during which time he told of the shooting...."I shot Juan Telles because I saw no other way to protect my life," said Hathaway.

A story filed by Jack Lefler, Arizona Associated Press Bureau Chief, had this to say:

Tom Hall wound up the direct questioning by asking, "Jim, why did you kill Juan Telles?" Hathaway replied, "I couldn't see any other way to save my own life and maybe my folks," the rancher replied. Before Hathaway took the stand, his wife and Mrs. Whiteside (both) testified they saw the shooting from the pickup truck...they said he had not told them anything about any possible trouble...they had seen Telles at the ranch....but had not heard any of his purported remarks.

"Jim Hathaway Case Goes to Jury Today," read the headlines in the May 18, *Nogales International* that touted itself as a "Nogales Home Newspaper, Published Where Two Nations Meet." The story predicted a speedy verdict and a follow-up article confirmed that assessment:

Rancher found innocent in Sonoita murder case. A superior court jury of ten men and two women deliberated only 30 minutes in reaching its verdict. Hathaway, accused of the rifle-duel killing of his life-long friend, Juan Telles, last Feb. 16, heard the ruling with no visible show of emotion.

A short two months later Virginia died suddenly of a heart attack and Jim moved back to the mountain place in the Huachucas. He seemed to be haunted by the ghosts of the many people he had brought to justice over the years, ever alert to any possible threat. He finally agreed to take a rare trip and went to San Francisco to visit his old friend Bourn (Jerky) Hayne, former editor of the paper in Nogales who had accompanied Jim on many of his adventures. Jerky later told friends that, "All the time Jim was here, he sat in a corner with his back to the wall."

In the fall of 1954, Jim, Art Rodgers and some Mexican cowpunchers were rounding up cattle at the mountain place for sorting and shipping. There was a particularly wild and aggressive cow that they had been trying to catch. The gate to the

Jim Hathaway's mountain cabin, now under water at Parker Canyon Lake. 1934.
Photo courtesy Howard Hathaway.

main corral was open and the cow darted inside. When Jim ran to close the gate, the cow made a run for it and Jim tried to block her escape by standing in front of the gate, yelling and waving his arms the way cowboys do to intimidate cows and turn them away. Instead of being scared off, the cow charged Jim, threw him up in the air and landed on him stiff-legged, finally goring him with her short stubby horns. The following day the 62-year-old Hathaway passed away at a Tucson hospital.

In a poignant note Howard wrote, "So the man who in turn had pursued and evaded enemies seeking his demise for so many years had met his end because of the swift charge of a mad cow. Before my dad's funeral, I wandered off alone into the hills east of the house. At random, I stopped on a knoll, sat on the ground and looked off toward Peterson Peak. A breeze came along and made a soothing sound in the dry fall grass. I fancied the spirits of my dad and mom riding free with the wind over the country they loved so well."

Ruins of the Gattrell house in Sunnyside. Gattrell was an old miner who sent away for a mail order bride from Germany. When she arrived, the head of the community, Mr. Donnelly, took a look at her and said to Gattrell, "The Lord has sent her out here for me, not you." Sam and Alvine Donnelly were married May 4, 1893 at Fairbanks, Arizona. Gattrell later married a schoolteacher, Diana Ely. Mrs. Gattrell had a drifter named Joe add the adobe fireplace to the house in the 1920s.
Barr photo

John McIntyre

Sunnyside

The ghost town of Sunnyside started out as a small religious community of miners founded by Samuel Donnelly, rumored to be a reformed patron of the bars in San Francisco. He became a preacher and leader of a group known as the Donnellites, relocated the Copper Glance Mine and established the town of Sunnyside in 1887.

John McIntyre's family moved to Sunnyside when he was a small child and helped to build the town. In later years, McIntyre and his wife, Anna, moved back to the site as caretakers and lived there until his death in 1985.

May and John Gates of the Heady Ashburn Ranch in the San Rafael Valley conducted Easter Sunrise Services for many years at Sunnyside and among the regulars was Dr. Paul Duffey of Tucson. Duffey penned the following poem upon "Uncle John's" death (reprinted with permission).

Memories of Uncle John McIntyre
© By Paul Duffey

He was born in Dodge City, Kansas, in 1891
Moved to Sunnyside, Arizona, when he was past one.
He left home at 13, not wanting to be a miner –
Returned at seventy, thought nothing could be finer

Than to finish his life where he'd lived as a kid
In the Huachuca Mountains, above Parker Canyon hid.
Keeping track of the place, all done with his roaming,
The schoolhouse, windmill, friend's homes in the gloaming.

We met John and Anna on a picnic we planned
Guided there by Blain Lewis, a Patagonia man,
With Mazie Gates, from Sonoita come down,
It was a long drive – a fur piece from town.

Anna and John were as friendly as could be
We ate our lunch with them in the shade of a tree
That John himself planted 65 years ago
Near the windmill that toppled this year in the snow.

The windmill was built nigh on seventy year ago
A marvel of construction as windmills go
By J. W. Guthrie, a man with a talent
With boards, sweat, nails and mallet.

The old windmill had stood, sturdy and tall,
For a good many years, wood ladder and all.
The schoolhouse is still there where John's father taught,
Where Blain and John learned what they ought.

The apple tree blossoms gave us some shade
To keep us cool while we drank lemonade.
Sandwiches, chips, fruit and surprise!
Mazie had baked her famous pecan pies.

John sat in the shade in his blue stocking cap
His dog waited patiently not far from his lap
For his chance to eat, when the diners missed the table
Letting some food drop, he'd grab some when able.

Betty Barr

John's face was deep line, a beard mid-length white
His blue eyes they twinkled, his memory bright,
He welcomed the visitors on Saturday and Sunday,
He looked forward to resting weary bones on Monday.

He cherished the old town his family helped build
To survive in that place he had to be strong willed.
For in Sunnyside they lived without modern utilities,
He lived without fanfare in kindly humility.

He was gentle in manner and soft-toned in voice,
He lived a good example for his Lord, Rejoice!
To witness his faith in his life was his choice
He touched many lives within sound of his voice.

He was rich in spirit, without any fortune amassing.
Somehow it seems fitting that the day of his passing
In his ninety-fourth year occurred on Good Friday.
To Anna "I love you" was the last he did say.

We'll all miss Uncle John, his spirit and smile,
At the old-timers reunion we'll all pause awhile,
And try to remember our dear long-lived friend
Who finally has passed beyond that great bend.

May God rest his soul in a place of great beauty,
Where the breezes are gentle, the aroma quite fruity,
If he has a choice, I know out of pride,
He'd pick a place that looks like Sunnyside!

Ruins of the Langford house at Sunnyside.
Barr photo.

Biff Lamma

Sunnyside and Patagonia

The little house nestles at the foot of one of the largest cottonwoods in Patagonia. It is said that it takes six big men with hands outstretched to girdle the trunk of the huge specimen and it is so impressive that the house seems almost an afterthought. Step through the threshold though, and the residence is revealed as a true gem from days gone by.

This charming house has been the home of Roberta "Biff" Lamma since her marriage to Frank in 1933. It was hauled to Patagonia after World War I when the Hardcastle Mine flooded out. The living room is completely paneled in tongue and groove, walls, floor, even the ceiling, giving the small room the feeling of a cozy nest. It was originally equipped with a three-burner coal oil stove, an old-fashioned icebox, and best of all, running cold water. Frank's dad was the pumper for the railroad, and with his help they ran water from the station across the way into the kitchen. Like most folks they also had a well in the back, but Biff felt very "up-town" because she didn't have to haul water into the house.

The east wall of the living room is a virtual gallery of art devoted to the subject of Sunnyside, Biff's home from the age of 14 months until her marriage. Hanging here is a collection of beautiful paintings, mostly originals with a scattering of prints, by artists whose names are instantly recognized locally: Herb Woods, Channing Smith, Emma Baldwin, Katheryn Drummond, Donna Soest and Lou Apperson, among others. Whenever Biff hears of a new rendering on the subject she immediately snaps it up for her "Sunnyside Wall."

Sunnyside is a ghost town today, but in its heyday it was a thriving mining camp with about 80 residents. In 1880 the Copper Glance was operated by two partners, Sam Donnelly and Alvin Gattrell, and was located near the Montezuma Pass on the southwest slope of the Huachucas, about seven miles east of Parker Lake. A sawmill was eventually built at what is now the site of Sunnyside, and the mine itself was five miles further up the canyon.

When the crew lived at the mining camp, they took the ore by burro over the mountain to Fairbanks for shipment and purchased their provisions at the market there. There were two large buildings at the camp with a kitchen in each, and the meals were served in relays. The rest of the camp was a tent city. When the mine flooded out in 1901, all the miners moved down to Sunnyside where they had built a dining hall large enough to seat 100. John McIntyre used to tell what a thrill it was to sit down together for their first meal in this kitchen at Christmas and not have to eat in shifts.

Mr. Donnelly was a religious man and according to Biff's mother, Laura Nye, he had memorized the entire Bible and could quote scripture to back up everything he said. Donnelly would preach to the people every evening and twice on Sunday, accompanied by the wonderful musicians in the camp. There were no saloons or anywhere to go for entertainment, giving Donnelly a captive audience; he boasted a 90% conversion rate.

In the meantime, the crew had to travel back and forth between the lumber and mining camps each day. Soon they started building one-room cabins - 18 in all. They would cook and eat in the dining hall and go to the cabins to sleep. With the coming of the railroad, the sawmill operation suffered badly. There were no streams to float lumber down to the sawmill so the logs all had to be snaked in, and they had to go farther and farther away for raw materials. Finally the sawmill was forced to discontinue, the workers left to find other employment and Sunnyside was deserted.

When Arizona became a state in 1912, Gattrell homesteaded at Sunnyside. His dream was to get all the people from the mining days to come back to work on what was now a cattle ranch. The only two families to return were the Langfords, who had lost their squatter's rights near Fairbanks, and Biff's mother, who by now was a young widow with two small daughters. The Nye family had been living in Phoenix when the father died leaving Laura with a bushel basket of debts and no skills. With no relatives west of the Mississippi to turn to, she used his carpenter's insurance to pay their debts, packed up their few possessions and returned to Sunnyside.

They moved into one of the little cabins and each morning Biff's mother would go down to the dining hall early to start the fires and get the breakfast ready for the cowboys and their families. She worked very hard for their keep and the only cash they had was the $30 a year she earned as assistant to Mrs. Langford, the postmistress. That paid for their clothes and medical emergencies.

Biff went to the one room school at Sunnyside. She was enrolled at the early age of four so there would be enough children to make up a class. They would push her up or put her back so there wouldn't be too many in one grade. Biff figures she only had two good years of grade school, one of high school and one of college. In spite of what Biff considers a hit or miss early education she has become a noted author-

The one-room school at Sunnyside, attended by Biff Lamma in the 1920s.
Photo courtesy Hathaway family.

ity on southeastern Arizona and has written several articles and an authoritative book on Sunnyside's history.

One of Biff's favorite stories was related in an article she wrote, "Law Enforcement Patagonia Style." Before the town had a proper jail, when someone got drunk or rowdy, the officer of the law would leg cuff him to what was called the Jail Tree. Many of the mesquites and cottonwoods that lined the main street were used this way. One day Manuel Haros was shackled to a mesquite tree on Smelter Avenue behind the Community Church. When it came time to release him all that was found were the remnants of a tree limb - his mother had sawed off the branch and taken him home!

When it came time for high school, Biff went to Patagonia and lived for three years with Buck Blabon and his wife, working for her room and board. Buck owned the Eastside Garage, incongruously located on the north side of town (its location has changed several times since then), and always had a kid from school working for him. At this particular time the kid was Frank Lamma, destined to be Biff's future husband and eventually the owner of the garage as well.

Biff's memories of her early married life in Patagonia centered around a little band that Frank had organized while he was still in high school. He played the drums, Jack Turner played the guitar, violin and trumpet and they had a "passing parade" of piano players. Every weekend, Biff and Frank were the first ones to arrive and the last to leave the local dances. They played at the San Rafael Schoolhouse, Sonoita Schoolhouse, the old Opera House (all gone now) and the Elgin Club. After about ten years Frank had enough of it and said the only way to get out of the band was to sell his drums, which he finally did.

After 21 years of marriage, the Lammas found to their astonishment that they were expecting a baby. Because of her age and petite size the doctor was very pessimistic and Biff didn't even buy any baby clothes. All the churches in town prayed for the little mother-to-be and happily the doctor was proven wrong. The baby is grown up with four children of her own and Biff now boasts of a great grandchild!

Betty Barr

The apple tree blooms every year even though the orchard has been deserted for
a long time.
Barr photo

Apple orchard

Sunnyside

Paul Duffey, physician and poet, attended a picnic in Sunnyside in 1985 and was struck by the oddly shaped apples growing in the orchard. He wrote this poem about the sheep-nosed apples (reprinted with permission). Duffey says, "Although I wrote this in the first person, the real nephew of Uncle Jess is Dolan Ellis, Arizona's State Balladeer."

Uncle Jessie's Apple Tree
© By Paul Duffey

My Uncle Jessie Hyatt had a farm in Ioway,
With an apple tree that's still growing today.
This story I will tell you about that special tree
And how these funny looking apples came to be.

Uncle Jess was plowing with his horse and iron plow
When he came upon a sapling he couldn't allow.
Thought he, I don't want a tree in my field
I'll simply plow it under, and it will yield.

He cut it off above the root, but didn't pull it out.
But lo, the next year again the sapling did sprout.
He plowed it twice this time to be sure
This little sapling tree would not endure.

And when a third year the sapling did appear,
He decided he and his plow wouldn't interfere.
He thought, "A wiser one than me must know
A good reason why this tree must grow."

And so he plowed around instead
And allowed this little tree a bed.
It grew and in its time produced
Nice apples ready to be juiced.

Uncle Jess picked peck after peck,
And when he looked, said "What the heck?
These apples all have sheep-like faces,
Each dented in, in the same several places."

Now a man named Mr. Stark of nursery fame,
Heard of these apples with special acclaim.
He gave Uncle Jessie some goodly pay
To take many cuttings from his tree away.

Eight years later a boy in Sunnyside
Planted some apple trees with pride
From the catalogue his father had ordered.
With Mr. Stark's trees, the meadow he bordered.

Many years later, Jess's nephew (that's me!)
Sat in Sunnyside under an old apple tree.
When I looked at the fruit I had to exclaim
"Those are sheep-face apples of Iowa fame!"

Betty Barr

When John McIntyre told me how they'd arrived,
With detective deductions, I soon had contrived
A story of how the sheep-nosed apples had come
From Iowa to Sunnyside via Mr. Stark, by gum!

The apples are delicious. I've had apple pie
From the apple tree that was too hardy to die.
So if in your life, you're ready to quit,
Bring this tale of sheep-nosed apples to wit.

And remember that strong persistence can win,
Being steady and sturdy, take it on the chin.
Ignore the world and its burdens of strife,
Follow the plan God made for your life.

May Gates, in dress and heels, teaches Sunday School to a group of rural children in her living room at the Heady-Ashburn Ranch in the mid 1950s. Photo courtesy May Gates.

Mary Bowman, May Gates and Marie Schorr

Leather, lariats and lace

"I always took a shower, dressed and put on heels and hose before I drove to Auntie Hogan's about 12 miles away, to meet the children at the school bus," reminisces May Gates about her life at the Heady Ashburn Ranch. The San Rafael Valley in the late 1940s was in the midst of a legendary drought and to coin a phrase, "out in the middle of nowhere," but rancher's wives in mid-century America never forgot their femininity. As May recalls, "One day I was all dressed up waiting for the bus, and this big limousine drove up. A man came up and rapped on the door and when he saw me he said, "My God, what are you doing living all the way out here?" May told him, "I like living here, it's close to God." His response: "Let's face it. There's no one out here **but** God."

May came to Arizona in 1944 with her husband John to manage the Vaca and Heady Ashburn Ranches. The owner of the Vaca, Mr. Weatherhead, never hired a manager unless he lived with him for a week, so he flew in from Ohio and they met him at a guest ranch in Patagonia. "We went riding and he had a wonderful horse that I rode. He thought I was quite a rider, but it was really that it was a great horse." The Gates were at the Vaca for seven years before moving to the Heady Ashburn where they ran 650 head of cattle on the two spreads.

Some of their first friends were Marie and Wag Schorr who came to Canelo in '49. Marie says, "I remember one day May and I went to Tucson for rodeo days and you were supposed to dress up in western attire. We ranchers wore that kind of clothes every day and when we went to town we got all dolled up in suits, gloves, hats and high heels. We had lunch at the Pioneer Hotel (which has since burned down) and when we came out, two vigilantes slapped on handcuffs and put us into a paddy wagon. They said we had to buy $10 rodeo tickets, but we had spent all our money on lunch. Finally they made us sing "Don't Fence Me In," and before we even got to the chorus they let us out to shut us up, I think."

Another longtime friend, Mary Bowman, moved to a ranch on the Greaterville Road in 1955 with husband Bob. She piped in, "Bob was on the board of the Elgin Club when Mrs. Everhart, who was president at the time, said that they would have to do something about the women coming to the dances in pants that are too tight. Bob and another board member were appointed to see a lawyer in Nogales about this very serious matter and reported back that if the person manning the door couldn't get a hand in the hip pocket of the pants, the woman would have to go home."

Wag Schorr purchased a ranch in Canelo in 1949, but Marie had never seen it. They drove out from Pennsylvania in a station wagon with their four boys and, "We were told at the gas station in Benson that we couldn't go any further, the roads were washed out, but we finally made it to Canelo about 11 a.m. I looked around and there were beer cans stacked everywhere. I didn't even want to get out of the car. The cowboy came over to the car and said he had told everyone that the dudes were arriving so they had a big party the night before. His wife was making tortillas on a wood stove. I had never seen a tortilla before, and we had beans, another first. We went in the house and when I turned on

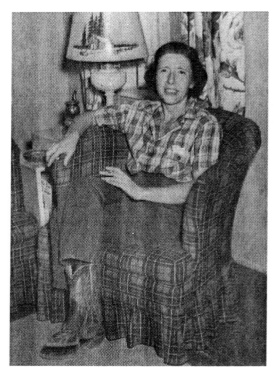

Marie Schorr relaxes at home, sporting her favorite pair of cowboy boots. Circa 1960s.
Photo courtesy Marie Schorr.

the tap in the kitchen the water just poured out. The pipes had frozen and weren't hooked up under the sink. I asked Wag if he didn't notice that when he looked at the property and he told me he was only looking at the ranch."

Things weren't much more modern when Mary and Bob Bowman arrived in 1955. They saw a property they liked but had to catch a plane back to California, so they sent a letter addressed to "Sonoita Chamber of Commerce" to inquire about a purchase. Mary chuckles to think about the reaction of Postmistress Hettie Lee Gardiner, who forwarded the missive on to Bum Hedgecock where it promptly ended up in the garbage.

Receiving no reply, the Bowmans decided the only thing to do was return in person and they hooked up with Tucson realtor Bill Fraesdorf who was well known as a ranch specialist. His wife, Marie, was the first weather woman on Tucson TV. "When we moved in we had a small TV set and the first night we were looking at it and Marie Fraesdorf came on and said, "If Bob and Mary Bowman are listening tonight, please get in touch with Marie and Wag Schorr. They are anxious to meet you."

According to May, "A rancher's wife was always busy. I would cook for the cowboys in the morning and then John would say, 'Honey, would you come and help round up some cattle?' Mary remembers that she used to vaccinate, until her eyes failed and, "I didn't want to hit them in the wrong spot!" And Marie was the counter. "You have to be careful to count how many bulls there are," she laughs.

In the late 70s when prices for cattle were at an all time high, Bob told Mary he wanted to serve steak at the roundup, and she decided to cook them all medium well. "Well, the buyer always liked to be in the kitchen and he came in and asked if we were having steak. I told him yes, because we were getting such a good price for the calves (a little slip of the tongue). Anyway, he asked if we had anything else because he couldn't chew too well and I brought out some leftover meatloaf. Wag Schorr came in and said, "Did I hear meatloaf?" According to Marie, he never wanted anything pink. All the old-timers would put the meat in a skillet, pat it down, and turn it over and over until it was completely ruined – that's the way they liked it. The meatloaf was the hit of the roundup.

For the first 14 years she lived in Canelo there was no electricity or phone service, according to Marie. The post office was the main source of communication. Ed LeGendre had the mercantile store in Sonoita and also served as the postmaster. He had slots for the mail behind the counter and, invariably, he read all the post-

Anthony Quinn (left) star of "Last Train from Gun Hill" with Bob and Mary Bowman of the Backward B Spear Ranch in Greaterville, during filming at the Empire Ranch in 1959.
Photo courtesy Bob and Mary Bowman.

cards. On one occasion, someone inquired about purchasing a cord of wood and when LeGendre read it he thought, "That's too high." He put a note on the bottom of the card stating that he could get the cord for $10 less.

Phone service came later and was even less private. As May remembers, "We had a wall phone that you had to crank up and there were about eight or ten people on the same line. Many times I would be talking and a third party would butt in and add their two cents worth to the conversation."

With such a lack of communication, country folk would just pop in on each other. May says, "John would come in and say he'd like to go to Schorr's for dinner. So I'd make a pie and we'd shower and drive over the Pass and say, 'Here we are.' Marie would throw a few more beans in the pot and we'd have an impromptu family gathering. That was the kind of life we all lived out here."

All three women have spent many hours in the saddle, suffered painful injuries, prepared thousands of roundup meals, doctored children and animals, taught Sunday school, raised vegetables and plants and performed countless hours of community service all in a remote area that even in the middle of the twentieth century was an outpost of the old west. They all agree on one thing however. As Mary says so well, "All my life, this is what I wanted to do. I am very grateful." "I never thought of it as work, it was just something that Wag dreamed of – he was a cowboy at heart," Marie adds. And May sums it up this way: "In these wide spaces you can keep your perspective. You take time to feel the stillness."

Robert Canady and his wife, Flora Belle, in 1925 with their three oldest boys, Tom, Bob
and Bill.
Photo courtesy Willis Canady

Willis Canady

Sonoita

A one-eyed mule, a second-hand wagon and a brand of "True Grit" that rivals John Wayne's, propelled Robert Canady and his four motherless boys from Gale, Illinois, to Arizona in the depths of the Depression years. His youngest child, Will, was only three years old when wife Flora Belle succumbed to "white plague" or tuberculosis. Eighteen months later the desperate and nearly destitute father loaded his children onto a homemade cart mounted on two cultivator wheels and pushed and pulled it two miles to Thebes, where they crossed the Mississippi on a ferryboat. He purchased a mule for $5, and a few miles farther on he squandered another $10 from his hoard, acquiring a proper wagon, which he fitted out with bow straps for the covering. The trip to a dry, healthy climate in a covered wagon pulled by a blind mule, was now underway in earnest.

Son Will, who grew up on Bill Douglass' ranch on the Greaterville Road near Sonoita and attended the one room Sonoita School in the late 1930s, has vivid recollections of that historic trek, even though he was only five years old at the time. His larger-than-life father, (at 6'4" he assumed heroic proportions) is remembered as a kind, loving, musical and spiritual man who had himself been orphaned at nine months of age and would do whatever it took to ensure that his boys would always stay together as a family. When he realized that TB was claiming him and his son,

Bill, he made the decision to relocate to the dry Arizona climate even though he didn't have the funds to purchase an automobile for the 2,000-mile journey.

Will still has the yellowed, crumbling remains of a small spiral notebook that his father used as a log to record their daily progress. From the first entry to the last, the journal reads like a saga from the early pioneer days:

> "Left Gale, Ill. 22 Sept., 1930
> Crossed Mississippi at Thebes
> Got mule 24 Sept. Illmo
> Bought wagon Rockview"
> Several days later the notations:
> "Crossed Arkansas River 30 Oct.
> Red River Toll bridge 8 Nov.
> Texarkana now in TEXAS!
> Fort Worth Thanksgiving Dinner (Chamber of Commerce)
> San Angelo, Christmas Dinner"
> A few pages farther on:
> "7 Jan. Ft. Stockton (Camped in jail-house)
> Deming, NM, 29 Jan.
> Bowie, Arizona, Feb. 4
> Texas Canyon, Feb. 8"
> Finally the entry:
> "Arrived Tucson, Arizona, 12 February 1931".

These cryptic notes give only a glimmer of the hardships and the joys experienced by the small family on their voyage. Will remembers his dad hanging an old tire on the back of the wagon for him to swing on. The mule was plugging along at a brisk clip when the rope frayed and the toddler was unceremoniously dumped in the roadway. Luckily an alert older brother noticed him bawling in the road and ran back to rescue him and the makeshift swing.

According to Will, Maude was surefooted despite her handicap. With one eye missing entirely and the other blind, she had developed a sixth sense, and trotted confidently ahead without much human direction. The only time he remembers her having a problem was when they reached an area in Texas where the roads were paved in red brick. They had to go up and over a railroad embankment and Maude misjudged the footing, slipped and fell. Undaunted, she hopped back up and continued on her way.

They covered about 20 miles a day, camping out in bedrolls under the wagon at night, usually close to the railroad tracks. Robert could tell from the railroad (RR) signs how far he had traveled and the distance to the next town and used this information for his journal notations. There were a lot of hobos on the rails, but the family was more leery of the many gypsy caravans they encountered. Robert had heard their reputation for thievery.

In East Texas they picked up two hitchhikers that were destined to become family pets. Affectionately known as Amos and Andy the furry creatures were seen scurrying under their wagon when a visitor was talking to Robert. The man asked if they were the boys' puppies and Robert, not wanting to lie, replied "That's Amos and Andy." The visitor was quoted in the local paper as having seen the cute puppies, never realizing they were skunks.

The Canadys' pioneering spirit and optimism in the face of hardship was well chronicled along their route. An article in the January 29, edition of the *El Paso Times* was titled, "Old Blind Mule Pulls Covered Wagon With Sick Cargo to West and Health". The following year, William R. Matthews, noted publisher of the *Arizona Daily Star*, wrote about their journey and eventual camp in Tucson, and a second article by Don Phillips ran in the same paper several years later. More recently, Bonnie Henry featured the family in her book, "Another Tucson" in a chapter titled "Canadyville".

To make ends meet along the way, the small family would pick cotton, make primitive tools and household items, collect cooking wood on the roadside, shoot rabbits for food, and even beg a meal from warmhearted farm wives. One time they went 30 hours without water. Young Bob saw a junked car in a pasture, went through the fence, and drained some water from the engine to quench their thirst.

Upon reaching Tucson they set up camp, later called Canadyville, on an empty lot west of town on Congress Street, near the Santa Cruz River. Robert eked out a living selling handmade chairs and flower stands that he fashioned out of wood harvested along the banks of the river. He was a preacher, played the banjo, and composed music. He is thought to be the author of "Cool, Cool Water," made famous by the Sons of the Pioneers, with the name changed from Maude to Dan. A proud man, Robert would never accept charity (although the local Kiwanis Club wanted to help out) and insisted that his boys stay together no matter what calamity befell them. According to Will, the longest any one of them was ever separated from the others was when the Western Boot Company of Tucson sponsored him to go to camp in the Chiricahua Mountains for a week.

Maude was happily out to pasture when Robert hitched her up again so he and the boys could go back east to settle a property claim. They got as far as Big Spring, Texas, when Robert became too ill to continue, so they sold Maude and hopped a freight train back to Tucson and Canadyville. Robert died in 1935 with his admonition, "Always stay together as a family," ringing in the boys' ears.

And stay together they did, for the rest of their lives. Bob was 16, and old enough to go out on his own, but the three younger boys were declared orphans and sent out to Bill Douglass' ranch in Gardner Canyon to live and help out with the chores. Will got off to a rocky start on his first day at the ranch when he spied an old gunnysack and decided to take a look. He peeked inside, imagined that he saw a snake, and yelled bloody murder. His brother leaped to the rescue by dropping a huge boulder on the sack, smashing two gallon-jugs of moonshine from Douglass' still.

The kids helped out with branding, de-horning, round-up and raising vegetables, but their main duty was milking the Holsteins. There were 32, including the bull, and Willis' brother used to tease him, "Yeah, you always milked the 32nd one." They used a separator and fed the milk to the dogs, chickens, pigs and turkeys, and then took the cream to the dock at Sonoita for shipment to Phoenix. Sometimes they would get tablets from the Watkins traveling salesman. They would put a #6 tub on a chair with a kerosene lamp underneath, mix a couple of tablets and hot salt water, pour it in with the milk and start stirring. After a while they would have the best cheese you ever tasted. There was a lot to learn and the slightest misstep brought swift and severe punishment, yet, in later years Will credits Douglass with "knocking some sense into my head, and helping me to become a man."

After a few months at Douglass Ranch, brother Bill joined the Civilian Conservation Corps (CCC) and was sent to Colorado. He eventually returned to cowboy at the Curly Horse Ranch, where he met and married Geraldine Kemp who was also working there. TB claimed his life at the early age of 23. Brothers Tom and Bob headed for Yuma to work for the railroad and Will says, "Zoom, this little guy followed them." Although Will was only 15 at the time, Bob signed that he was 18 so he could join the CCC. Later, the brothers joined the Marines and served in WWII, where Will survived combat three times. At the end of the War, the three settled in the Tucson area and, remaining true to their father's admonition always kept in close contact with each other.

Robert Canady's courageous spirit illuminated the path his sons followed through life. Although Will had the benefit of Robert's parenting for only nine years, the strength of this early influence is obvious. Despite the lack of a formal high school education, Will learned a lot in the CCC and the Marine Corps and studied aerodynamics, meteorology and radio under the GI Bill. He earned a pilot's license in 1947 and went on to work for the FAA for 21 years. His many achievements are a testimony to his remarkable father who instilled a love of family and pride of individual accomplishment in his four boys.

Henry Dojaquez and Willis Canady

The CCC – a lifeline for Depression-era youth

They were known as the "CCC Boys," and boys they were. The minimum age was 18, but many, such as Henry Dojaquez and Willis Canady, fudged a little to snag one of the coveted positions. They were only 16 or 17 years old when they set off for a six-month tour at a CCC Camp. The chance to earn $5 a month and send another $25 home to help the family was a godsend to poverty-stricken households in the throes of the Depression.

Over 3 million young men enrolled in the Civilian Conservation Corps from its inception in 1933 until it was disbanded in June1942. The CCC was organized like a military operation, except that the boys signed up for six months instead of a two-year tour of duty. The recruits were sent off to live in a camp with other youths and lend their muscle to the federal effort to conserve our forests, farms and wildlife. The Army ran the barracks and the Forest Service was in charge of the work details. The boys were provided with medical care, clothes and three squares a day. Many had never been so well fed and it's said the average boy gained 11.5 pounds in his first three months of duty.

Sometimes known as "Roosevelt's Tree Army," the CCC crews planted literally millions of trees, and built fire trails, campsites, and roads in many of Arizona's national parks and across the country. Most of the work was done by hand, using picks, hoes, axes and shovels. Along with the hard work came an education (it is estimated that over 40,000 illiterate youths learned to read) and on-the-job training in skills that would transfer to paying jobs in the civilian world.

Dojaquez started out in a camp in Flux Canyon near Patagonia in 1933. His crew was assigned the job of building ranch fences in the Patagonia area and they also constructed the old adobe ranger station near where Patagonia High School now stands. In early 1934 Henry was sent to a camp in the Chiricahuas to help build roads, a visitor's center and the Massai Point Lookout Tower. They ran water lines from a spring at the top of Rustler's Park and built the roads, cutting the curves with the aid of a special "dump truck" commonly known as a wheelbarrow. The miles of beautiful hiking trails still in use in the Chiricahuas today are a testament to their hard work.

Henry, whose love of a good joke is well known in the Sonoita area, spent 18 months in those mountains, but "left" rather abruptly several months before his last tour was to end. One of the other boys was a pretty irritating character. Finally one day Henry picked him up by the heels and plunged him headfirst into a water tank. At that point, it seemed like a good idea for Henry to return to civilian life!

For Canady, getting into the CCC was his golden opportunity to escape from the state foster care system and be reunited with his brothers. Willis had arrived in Tucson at the age of five with his widowed father and three brothers. They had made the trip in a homemade wagon pulled all the way from Illinois by a blind mule. A few years later his father succumbed to tuberculosis and the orphaned boys were sent to live and work on Bill Douglass' ranch in Gardiner Canyon.

By 1941 the older brothers had already enrolled in the CCC and, with their help, Willis was somehow able to convince the authorities that he too was 18. His first assignment was in Yuma, where he became a tool room clerk and later he was sent to a camp in Glenwood, New Mexico. Although he only spent a year in the program before it was dissolved in 1942, he credits this early training, along with his military service in WWII, with providing him the skills and education he would need in later life.

The camaraderie of the CCC boys was strong and both Henry and Willis have retained a lifelong association with some of their buddies from those days. They have attended a reunion that the Forest Service hosts honoring the hard work and determination of these less-chance boys whose efforts beautified our forests and made them readily accessible to the public.

In 1993, Congress created a national program patterned along the lines of the old CCC called AmeriCorps. It employs youths in projects that conserve natural resources and also offers training in disaster relief and recovery projects. The program is open to youths 18 – 24, willing to commit to 11 months of service. They receive lodging, meals, and job skill training along with a living allowance.

Lyle Sprung's draft horses pulling a wagon with metal wheels. Early 1930s.
Photo courtesy Russell Sprung

Sprung family

Sonoita

Russell Sprung, whose family homesteaded on the Curly Horse Ranch Road in the early 1900s, has many tales to tell. His dad, Lyle Sprung, became a Forest Ranger in the days when a man could ride all the way from Mt. Baldy to the Whetstones without ever hitting a fence. Lyle discovered a spring on Mt. Baldy, now known as Sprung Spring, a tongue twister that puzzles hikers trying to decide if the name derives from some obscure physical phenomenon.

Grandfather Sprung settled on the Curly Horse Road property in 1912. The homestead laws required a 12' x 14' house, so he constructed a tarpaper dwelling where the family lived while he added on a mud adobe building. Russell's mother, Dorothy Putnam, came to the area with her family in 1910.

Lyle Sprung spent a good part of his life in the Santa Ritas and pastured his horses near the Mt. Baldy cabin. When the last big blizzard hit the area, in November of 1958, a group of Boy Scouts who had been camping there were lost in the snowstorm. Lyle, who by that time was retired, went to the sheriff and offered to help guide a rescue party, but they refused his offer saying that they had plenty of people who knew the area just as well as he did. They must have thought an "old fella" would hold them back. As it turned out, their experts had recently arrived from back east and had never been off the trail before. Lyle had told his son that if he were trapped up there he would try to head down toward MacBeth Springs. When the spring thaws came, that's where the bodies of the three missing scouts were discovered.

Lyle also delivered the mail by horseback to the Greaterville area. He finally gave up the route and when Russ asked him why, he said it was because of Sears Roebuck. When the new catalogs came out they weighed about 20 pounds! The Greaterville area attracted a lot of colorful characters. Russ's Uncle Harold Guyon lived at Kentucky Camp with Wick Fenter and had a heated argument with Jack Doyle earlier in the day over a mining claim. As he and Wick were playing cards that evening, the door suddenly flew open revealing Jack Doyle brandishing a gun. Harold threw the lamp at him and Jack shot Uncle Harold in the forearm, taking off most of the flesh and nicking him in the chest. He appeared to be dead.

Doyle pointed his six-shooter at Wick, marched him over to a tree and told him, "You put your hands against that limb and if you take them down, I'm going to kill you." Wick grabbed the branch and when he thought he heard Doyle leaving he started moving his hands down. He heard Doyle cocking that old six-shooter and jerked his hands back up automatically. He had a long ordeal before he got nerve enough to bring his hands down again, and by that time Doyle was long gone. Fenter rushed Uncle Harold down to Thurber's Ranch and they got him to a hospital, but he died soon afterwards.

Another adventure involved Mark Turney and Martin Wilson. The two were riding out in the Whetstones when they rode up too close to a squatter's house and one of the residents shot them both. Turney was badly wounded in the leg but managed to stay on his horse and ride for help. Wilson was hit in the chest, fell off his horse and landed in the creek-bed not far from the house. A young girl heard him hollering and came out of the house to help but her father dragged her roughly back inside. The sheriff's posse finally rescued Wilson, but Turney's leg could not be saved. The squatters left the state.

Russell says the best bronc rider he ever worked with was Dave Antrobus, commonly known as Cockeye. Cockeye rode for the Sands Ranch. One winter day Russ and Cockeye were driving some cattle. It was snowing and the mud was two or three inches deep. Cockeye was riding a cutting horse by the name of Peanut. The wind was blowing and when a couple of head broke and ran downwind, Cockeye galloped ahead to turn them back. Peanut, being a cutting horse, thought he was trying to cut this one animal and as Cockeye was riding through the group they got their signals mixed.

When the horse tried to correct, he slid in the mud and cartwheeled, end over end. Russell couldn't believe his eyes. He was seeing a cowboy ride a horse upside down; Cockeye's hat was right down next to the ground and the horse's hoofs were up in the air. When the horse rolled again, Cockeye left him. Russ says, "If he hadn't been a real top bronc rider he'd of never made it because the next time over, that saddle just buried itself in the mud."

Over on the Empire Ranch, the ramrod for a long time was Fred Barnett. One day he was gathering and got a loop on a two-year-old when suddenly, the horse and rider were going in different directions. It tore the horn right off his saddle and destroyed it. The next day the young cowboys went to a dance at the Elgin School and bought raffle tickets on a new saddle. "Lucky Fred" won the prize and got a replacement saddle for the grand sum of 50 cents.

Life in Sonoita wasn't all riding and roping. Russell attended the one-room Sonoita School, located at the Crossroads just north of the current post office building. Most of the teachers were normal school graduates who came west to find work during the Depression. These young ladies were quite entranced with cattle drives and cowboys and Russ remembers when his teacher decided to treat the class to a field trip to the stockyards. Nobody expected ladies and kids to be at the stockyards, so when one of the cowboys slid along the top bar of the fence and got a splinter in his thigh he just dropped his pants. The mortified teacher hurriedly gathered her charges and hustled them back to school, effectively ending field trips for a while.

When Russell was about 16, he got a job working for Dr. Klenne. He had only been to Tucson once or twice in his life and when Klenne and his wife offered to take him to town, he jumped at the chance. He enjoyed the morning buying new Levis and seeing the sights.

Along about noontime he went to Woolworth's lunch counter for a bite to eat. A big sign advertised, "Tuna sandwiches, 19 cents." He'd never had one before but it sounded good, so he ordered it. When it arrived and he took a bite, he thought it must be someone else's order. He called the waitress over and she looked at it and said, "That's what you ordered, tuna salad." Russ said, "But it tastes like fish."

The only tuna Russ knew about was nopal or prickly pear cactus. Commonly referred to as tuna, the pads of the cactus were considered a real delicacy by the rural kids. The amused waitress thought he was a real hick, but Russ still thinks his kind of tuna would have made a great sandwich.

Margaret Vail watches cowboys working cattle in the historic upper corral constructed of pole fencing. Ranch buildings in background. Large barn at left no longer exists. Pre-1885.
Photo courtesy Laura Vail Ingram and the Empire Ranch Foundation.

Vail family

Empire Ranch, Sonoita

It was early December 1914, and several murderers had been spotted near the Empire Ranch in Sonoita. The young rancher, Banning Vail, along with a group of deputies, had set out on the manhunt when word was received that Vail's first child was about to be born in Tucson. Leaving the posse, he hurried to town to welcome his daughter into the world. Vail laughingly observed that the baby must be thirsty, she was bawling so loudly she sounded "dusty." The nickname stuck, and as Dusty Vail often remarked, the name suited her a lot better than the ladylike, Laura, that she was christened with. It was later learned that the man who replaced Vail on the posse was killed and the family always credited Dusty with saving her father's life.

Growing up on a ranch in the early twentieth century was an exciting adventure for Dusty Vail Ingram, a little girl who idolized her dad and loved horses. The fearless tomboy was up on a horse at age six. One day when no one was around she lugged her saddle up on the fence, then dropped it down on the horse and hopped aboard. All went smoothly until she returned from the ride and leaned down to unlatch the gate. The horse shied and Dusty's foot caught in the stirrup. She was dragged a little way before the horse kicked her in the face, breaking some bones and laying her cheek open. The doctor felt an anesthetic might cause more swelling, so he sewed it up right away while he could still see the lip line. Her dad told her to pull his hair as hard as she could every time it hurt. He said, "Then you'll know it's hurting me as much as it is hurting you." Dusty felt her vigorous yanking might have contributed to his receding hairline in later years but the distraction helped, and once she healed there was no sign of the injury.

Far from letting this incident dampen her enthusiasm for riding the range, Dusty viewed it as her golden opportunity to get a better mount. It wasn't long before her father put her up on Coltee, his best cutting horse. She had no formal riding instruction -although years later she graduated from advanced equestrian instruction for calvary officers. Her dad said the best way for her to learn was watch and do what the horse suggested. "I can tell you a lot of things about working cattle, but your best teacher is this horse. Watch the ears and the horse will show you what to do."

Soon Dusty was out on the range helping with gatherings. When her younger brothers were old enough to sit a horse, they played cops and robbers and other games on horseback.. When the youngsters came upon a mountain lion in the cottonwoods not far from the ranch house, brother Bill kept his eye on the cat and Dusty galloped home to get a gun. The horses were spooked when the gun went off, but they finally quieted and the kids were able to drag the carcass back to the house.

The ranch that Dusty grew up on had been in the Vail family for about 40 years by the time she was born. Their first 160 acres was originally homesteaded by William Wakefield. He sold it in 1876 to his brother-in-law, E. N. Fish and a partner, Simon Silverberg, for $500. Less than two months later, the pair turned around and sold the parcel to Dusty's grandfather, Walter Vail, and his partner Herbert Hislop for $2,000 in U.S. gold coin. Hislop eventually returned to his native England and Vail, along with various other partners, continued to add to the holdings until by 1881 it was truly on the way to becoming an Empire, boasting more than 5,000 head of cattle and including the Total Wreck Silver Mine, a townsite of 300 residents and a toll road that controlled the cattle trail to the Southern Pacific loading chutes.

At this point, the prosperous rancher was in a position to make the trip to his home back east to claim his future bride. He had recently added a huge Victorian bay window to the house that he hoped would convince his fiancée's socially prominent family that he would not be bringing their daughter to a savage and uncivilized outpost. Walter Vail and Margaret Russell Newhall were married in Plainfield, NJ, and returned to the Empire where they lived until 1896 when they moved the headquarters to Los Angeles.

Vail had acquired ranches in California including Santa Rosa Island, now part of the National Park Service, but continued to travel back and forth to oversee the

The first car in Arizona, a 1904 Oldsmobile, pictured at the Empire Ranch. It was on its way to a parade in Bisbee for the hard rock drilling contest. Jim Seagar, superintendent of Helvetia Copper Mine in the background. Circa 1904.
Photo courtesy Empire Ranch Foundation and the Bureau of Land Management.

operations at the Empire. He was killed in a tragic accident in 1906 getting off a streetcar. He turned to help his wife disembark when another streetcar came along in the opposite direction and he was crushed between the two. His son, Banning, 17 years old at the time, was sent to Arizona to train at the Empire Ranch. In 1913 he became the manager.

Within the year, his heart was captured by the bright and vivacious Tucson native, Laura Perry, who despite the difficulty of being engaged to three other suitors at the same time, agreed to marry him and move to the Empire. As was the custom of the day, there were maids, cooks and nannies living at the headquarters and Laura's main responsibility was to oversee the smooth operation of the home and provide a comfortable atmosphere for their many guests.

Although she had ridden some as a child, she was not an accomplished horse-woman and always made the excuse that she couldn't go out on the range because she didn't have the proper riding habit. Finally, Banning and the children convinced her to order an outfit and she sent away for a pongee silk riding costume complete with high boots and a Panama hat.

Dusty remembered the outing as a miserable event. "Mother never stopped worrying about us children and finally we were on the way home and that was great. We came to a spring with a low reservoir and Mother leaned over to get a drink. I looked at Dad and there was a peculiar look in his eye so I thought maybe I'd get away with it. I gave her a very gentle push and she went in head over heels and came out like a drowned rat!" Once Laura got out of her wet clothes she had to laugh at the sight of a contrite Dusty parading by her window with a bouquet of wildflowers, the surefire way to gain forgiveness for any misdeed. The episode provided Laura with a wonderful excuse never to ride again – the pongee silk shrank and once again she had "nothing suitable to wear."

Laura soon became known for her wonderful hospitality and the ranch was always the site of a continual stream of visitors – friends, relatives and business associates, but to the impressionable youngster, the real magic of the Empire was the large cast of romantic characters who lived and worked there. There was Apache Joe, the stoic Indian whose job was to keep a continual supply of mesquite firewood on hand. He would stack it in huge piles and bring it up to the house as needed in an old wheelbarrow. The ranch hand, Bartolo, was the envy of the other cowboys because his wife rolled his cigarettes and put them in a metal box for him to take out on the range. Mr. Helmann was the prim and proper bookkeeper who kept track of all the cattle transactions and managed the ranch store, but still took the time every morning to clean all the canned goods with a feather duster.

Lena the cook had a beautiful Jamaican accent and little apple cheeks. Her children, Freda and Brother, were Dusty's favorite playmates. Lena first came to the ranch to work in the lower kitchen, cooking for the cowboys. She served them delicious jerky, frijoles and tortillas and the children were soon sneaking off to eat at that table. Lena's culinary talent became the talk of the ranch and soon she was moved to the upper kitchen to cook fancier fare for the family.

Dusty and her favorite playmate, "Brother" Brown, son of family cook,
Lena Brown. 1918.
Photo Courtesy Empire Ranch Foundation and Laura Vail Ingram.

Mr. Purofoy, the hard of hearing manager of the store at Pantano Station, could put messages through to the outside world, but when Mrs. Jones, the new cook, tried to give him a telegraph message, he had trouble understanding her German accent. When she got to the part notifying the recipient how many carloads of bulls the Empire had shipped, he just couldn't make out the word "bulls." Mrs. Jones tried spelling it for him to no avail and she finally said, "No, I said bulls! Bulls - the cows' husbands!"

Dusty (at three to four years of age) "driving" the locomobile at Empire Ranch, 1917.
Photo courtesy Empire Ranch Foundation and Laura Vail Ingram.

Dusty Vail

Empire Ranch, Sonoita

Laura (Dusty) Vail Ingram was born in Tucson in December 1914 and nick-named Dusty by her father, Banning Vail, who thought that the bawling baby sounded parched and thirsty. Her mother was Laura Perry, a Tucson native well-known and loved for her gracious hospitality. She kept the ranch filled with a large cast of romantic characters that Dusty remembered for the rest of her life.

The new nursemaid who arrived from across the border, was barefoot and had two children of her own. She had been beaten and abused by her husband and wanted to get out of Nogales so he wouldn't be able to find her. When they asked her name, she said she didn't want a Mexican name, and wanted Mrs. Vail to re-name her. Laura reeled off a list of names and the girl picked Sally. From that day forward she was known as Sally. Another favorite was the maid, Josefina Escalante, who would chase them with her broom when they would tease her with, "Josefina Escalante, color de elephante."

Ma and Pa Farrar lived in an old house out toward Rosemont Station, one of the outlying sections of the ranch. Ma had been pestering Banning that she needed a new house so they went out there to figure out where to build it. Banning insisted on a spot on the edge of a bluff, looking down on a wash even though Ma kept shouting that she wanted it built right next to her old house. In her old age, Ma fixed all their meals from cans. When she was done, she threw the empty cans out the window.

Banning said if he built it on the cliff she could throw the cans out, they'd roll down the hill, when the flash floods came they would all be washed away: an early day waste disposal system.

Dusty had no interest in helping around the house with domestic chores; she always wanted to be more like the cowboys. Wearing dresses, and especially bloomers, was the bane of her existence and it was a happy day when she was finally allowed to switch to blue jeans and chaps. Chaps available at the mercantile were too big and stiff for her to ride in comfortably. Somehow, Banning talked Blas "Shorty" Lopez, the ranch foreman, into letting her wear his "broken-in chaps." Shorty wasn't much taller than Dusty so it was the perfect solution. Her dad also had a saddle made for her at Porters, a well-known saddle making shop in Phoenix

Dusty wearing her "broken-in" chaps, hand-me-down from foreman, Blas "Shorty" Lopez. Circa 1925.
Photo courtesy of Empire Ranch Foundation and Laura Vail Ingram.

at the time and allowed her to trade in her traditional Mary Janes for a pair of lace-up shoes that came up above the ankle.

Her greatest joy was to hop on her horse for impulsive excursions. One day the family was eating lunch in the dining room and Banning mentioned that he'd love to have some watercress. There was a spring nearby that was lush with watercress, so Dusty tore down to the orchard on horseback, pretending she was the pony express, filled a lard bucket with the watercress and dashed back with it, proudly announcing, "Got the mail there on time."

Business was the heart of the ranch operation. When there were guests for dinner, the men would repair to the large bathroom off the master bedroom to smoke their cigars and talk cattle after dessert. They referred to it as the "Gentlemen's Room." Business had a way of interfering with the family's plans too. Many an eagerly anticipated trip to Tucson, with mother and the children waiting in the car, was delayed at the last minute when a cowboy would suddenly run up with a wire of ear cuttings. During branding, the cowboys would notch the calf's ear and spear the cutting on a piece of baling wire, giving an exact count on the number of calves they had processed. What this interruption meant to the kids was a one-to-two-hour wait, while Banning and the boys discussed the condition of the cattle and how many calves they had.

One year there were several springs on the property that needed to be cleaned out. A lot of trash had built up over time and it was getting harder for the water to get to the surface. When Banning got down near the bottom he found all kinds of cooking and eating implements, possibly dropped in the spring by people who had been dipping a cup for drinking water or washing dishes. A professor came down to the ranch from the University of Arizona and found an Indian burial site near the spring. The skeletons were all lying face down, leading the researchers to speculate that they had been killed in battle and buried in the prone position to make it harder for them to get up to the happy hunting ground.

Not long afterwards the Empire was sold to the Boice family's Chiricahua Cattle Company and at age 12 or 13 Dusty moved from the Empire. Her life as a "cowboy" was over forever. Almost 70 years later, Dusty Vail Ingram told an interviewer, "My formative years – really the most fun years of my entire life, were spent on the Empire. I don't know of anything that influenced me as much as the 12 years that I spent there on the ranch. They molded a great deal of my thinking and living – not only me, but my children as well. I often wonder how it's possible out of a whole lifetime of 80 years, that 12 years could have been so important. I certainly wasn't aware of what it meant to me (at the time) and that's the pity of it all. The most important thing is the legacy I passed on to my children."

Laura, "Dusty" Vail Ingram died April 17, 2003 at age 88 and was buried in Arlington National Cemetery next to her beloved husband, Navy Captain Red Ingram (Ret.). The Empire Ranch where she grew up is now part of the Las Cienegas Natural Conservation Area. She assisted with restoration and research projects relating to the ranch and helped establish the Empire Ranch Foundation. Several years before her death she remarked to interviewer, Will Woolley, "The Bureau of Land Management. I couldn't think of a better thing that could have happened to this ranch. (I foresee that) it will become available to many people with different pursuits (who will be able to) learn what the west was really about."

Betty Barr

Wagon boss, Fred Barnett (from left), and ranchers Mary and Frank Boice, 1949.
Photo courtesy Boice family and the Empire Ranch Foundation.

Boice family

Empire Ranch, Sonoita

The purebred Hereford is generally acknowledged as a breed well suited to thrive in inhospitable Arizona, but in the early part of the twentieth century most cattlemen were raising tough Spanish cattle. They were a hardy breed, surviving the extremes of temperature and poor forage, but did not produce much beef. One of the people most responsible for establishing a pure strain of Herefords in Arizona was Henry S. Boice, patriarch of the family destined to become the last private owner of the historic Empire Ranch in Sonoita.

Boice was born in Las Vegas, NM, in 1860. He began cowboying at age 15, earning the princely sum of $15 a month. He gained hands-on cattle experience and, through what is now called "total immersion," became fluent in Spanish as well. Thanks to the education provided by his physician father, he learned how to get along in business and was soon swinging cattle deals and arranging complicated financing. By the age of 21, he had risen to the position of foreman and then partner in the Creswell Ranch.

His interest in Herefords led him to Simpson & Gudgell in Independence, Missouri, breeders of the best Hereford bulls money could buy. There he met and married LuBelle Gudgell in 1891 and moved to Kansas City where they raised five children. They spent their summers in Colorado where sons Frank and Henry were thoroughly trained in cattle and ranch life. The boys were only five and six years old when they helped trail 2,000 heifers to Texhoma as full-fledged ranch hands. Their mother was a tough lady, according to her granddaughter, Peggy Boice Rupel. As a diehard Republican, she supported Thomas Dewey for president in 1948. But, Bess Truman had been a bridesmaid in her wedding, so she also wanted to vote for her old hometown friend, Harry. Although her family tried to convince her that it would negate her ballot, she went ahead and voted for both candidates anyway.

Boice later became general manager of the Chiricahua Cattle Company (CCC) in the Sulphur Springs Valley of southern Arizona. Chiricahua, pronounced quickly, sounds like cherry cows, and that was the name the cowboys always used. The name was changed in 1908 to Boice, Gates & Johnson, but everyone continued to call the huge operation the "Cherry Cows."

Boice started a purebred bull program on his San Carlos Indian Reservation allotment using the same methods that had worked well for him in the past. With 400 cows purchased from the XIT Ranch in Texas and his purebred Hereford bulls, he began a process of careful elimination and selection to achieve the highest quality range cattle. The XIT covered ten Texas counties, hence the name. X stood for ten, I for in and T for Texas.

Henry S. Boice died in 1919 and his 24-year old son, Henry Gudgell Boice took over. A few short years later the San Carlos Tribe cut off all permits to non-Indians and young Henry was faced with the prospect of moving 20,000 cows – the big question was not only how, but where? He and his brother Frank added to their operation near Pearce, purchasing four more ranches over the next six years: The Eureka near Willcox in 1924, the Empire and Rail X in the Sonoita/Patagonia area in 1928, and finally the Arivaca on the border southwest of Tucson. The benefits of these purchases soon became apparent: they covered a large area of the state, were widely scattered, minimizing the possibility of drought hitting all the ranges at once, and all four had Forest Service permits coupled with patented land.

It took five years to complete the move from San Carlos. As the steers came of age they were shipped to market and the cow herd was moved in lots on long cattle drives and roundups. The bubble burst around 1939 when the Forest Service limited the number of cows per lessee to 1,200 head. Rather than splitting up their leases, the Boices decided to sell the Eureka and parts of their other ranches. Henry Boice and his family took over the Rail X and Arivaca Ranches and Frank and Mary Boice ran the Empire.

Ranching on the Empire in the late 30s and 40s was done the old-fashioned way. Mary Boice participated in all facets of ranch life, including round-ups, sorting and shipping. "She did everything but doctor for screw worms," according to fellow rancher, Bob Bowman. In fact, Mary was well known around these parts as a "good hand." Jane Woods remembers her father, Stone Collie, remarking, "If you want a good job done (on the range), send Mary Boice."

Gordon Cooper, who cowboyed on the Empire during that era describes the old Porter's Saddlery Company in downtown Tucson, where a good saddle ran about $75. After the shop was locked up for the night, the door to an attic room would be left open and cowboys waiting to go to a ranch could roll out their bed and stay as long as a week, free of charge. The ranchers would come in when they needed hands and Porters would send the boys out. When Cooper and his cousin arrived there in late 1936, he was told, "Frank Boice is a good man to work for."

The hands would be issued five or six horses each when they arrived at the ranch. They were responsible for shoeing each horse with a special shoe they fashioned that they called a Chiricahua. It was shaped a little longer than the heel and then knocked down on the anvil till it would lay up the side of the hoof. With this design, it was easy for the horse to slide down the rocky hillsides.

Screwworm infestations were the scourge of the range and often each cowboy would rope four or five animals a day to doctor them. Calves were roped and dragged to the fire for branding, using manila ropes about 30 feet long. The Mexican cowboys used longer ropes that they dallied, but the other boys tied hard and fast.

Gordon and his cousin usually rode the rough string - horses that are hard to break. They buck and most cowboys refuse to ride them. On Gordon's first roundup at the Empire, Frank told him he had a nice cow horse named Trashy that no one could ride. He was what they called a brush horse. When you were holding up in brushy country these horses would turn their heads and twist and jig, and you would know the cattle were coming even before you could hear anything. A horse can't be trained to do this - it just comes naturally - and Trashy turned out to be one of the best.

The headquarters was a rock adobe building with a long breezeway in the center with hooks to hang the meat. It had screen nets and the wind could blow through. An old pensioner named Dee, was in charge of the storeroom and whenever anyone needed anything to eat they could go to Dee and he would dole it out. He knew all the horses, helped the cowboys out, and acted as a handyman around the place.

The cowboys would help make jerky. They would cut the meat in long pieces, spread it out on tables and pepper it so thickly it would look like flies had been on it, then hang it over a wire to dry. The crisp strips would be packed into flour sacks and sent out to camp where camp cooks would break it up with a hatchet, add water and make stew or fix it in a skillet with gravy and biscuits. The rest of their meal consisted of beans, potatoes and dried fruits.

For entertainment there were the weekend dances at the Elgin Club or the old Sonoita Schoolhouse. When the dance started the cowboys would get their "duty dances" out of the way and then the serious dancing and drinking would begin. The definition of "duty dance" translated to: "If you know what's good for you, you better dance with at least two or three of the hostess committee ladies and the daughters of your rancher friends who might be sitting on the sidelines, " according to Cooper.

Roundups at the Empire and Rail X were legendary. Some of the great wagon bosses were Dick Jimenez, Blain Lewis, Nacho Garcia and Fred Barnett to mention just a few. Two chuck wagons and two cooks would set up at the old stock pens in Sonoita, along with two straw bosses and 30 cowboys - all working together. The branding was done at the ranch but everything else, cutting, sorting and classifying, was done during the drive

The cows and calves were driven down together and then, still out in the open, the calves were cut off from the mothers. "This is difficult to do, because the calves would run over you, the cows would run over you. You had to be a horse buff, I'll tell you," Cooper recalls. At the last big shipment they had, the crew was there for an entire week shipping 75 carloads out of Sonoita. They would load up a train every day and it would make the delivery to Nogales, then return and pick up as many cars as were ready and make the trip again. Over a thousand head were shipped on that legendary final drive. Traces of the old railroad are still visible just south of the Sonoita Crossroads behind the Steak Out Restaurant.

After Frank's death, sons Bob and Frank, Jr., "Pancho," controlled the operation. The ranch was sold to Gulf American in 1960 and then resold to Anamax in 1976. It is now managed by the Bureau of Land Management in partnership with the Empire Ranch Foundation as part of the new Las Cienegas Conservation Area. John and Mac Donaldson run the cattle leases.

Betty Barr

Cowboy dragging a steer to the branding fire on the Empire Ranch.
Photo courtesy Laura Vail Ingram and the Empire Ranch Foundation.

Fred Sijarto

Cowboying across the county

Itchy feet started the "whole mess," according to Fred Sijarto. Fred and his roping buddy, Dean, two twenty-something guys, were knocking around dude ranches and weekend rodeos in New York and New Jersey, when they got the urge to go West and try their hand at real cowboying. The year was 1945, and Fred got hired on for the fall roundup at the Empire Ranch, working for Henry, Frank and Charlie Boice's Chiricahua Cattle Company (CCC).

Everything went smooth as glass as they trailed the cattle from the Empire to the shipping pens at Sonoita. Then the whole crew piled into a truck and went to the Arivaca Ranch, also owned by the CCC. "That's where we had a little problem."

The CCC, jokingly nicknamed the Cherry Cows, had little patience for wasting time. According to Fred, "There was no sleeping when the Cherry Cow sun was out." The cowboys called the moon, "the Cherry Cow sun," because they would start work before the sun came up and didn't quit until it was dark. Peggy Boice Rupel remembers, "One cowboy, Luis Romero, who had worked for the Cherry Cows at Arivaca most of his life, described his life as "I work all day for $1 and work all night to keep my job!"

"It was about a 20-mile two-hour round trip for the trucks to haul cattle from the Arivaca Ranch to the shipping pens in Amado. They couldn't take all the cows by truck so we had to trail the second bunch down. It was starting to get dark and there was a barbed wire fence on one side and a big wash to the left of us. The cattle were going down nice and calm and the cooks were already down at the holding pasture making supper. Suddenly somebody says, 'Hey, quit pushing them, I'm on a ledge out here and I can't go no further.' (sic) That's when it happened. The cattle came back running and we had a stampede. One of the fellas said, "I know where there's a low spot where we can jump off about four feet." So we bailed out and let the cattle go." When they finally got the cattle gathered up and down to the holding pasture, their reward was a chewing out from the irate cook. "He didn't take kindly to having to heat up the biscuits again."

The next morning they started out for the railroad yard at Amado. They got to the Nogales Highway, coaxed the cows to go across the pavement and then drove them in bunches past the little adobe houses in the town. "We're going down the dirt street and here's this one lady doing her laundry. She's got one of them (sic) pump washing machines and she cranks that thing up, whirrr, and the cattle spooked. They ran down to the railroad tracks, made a left turn and ran right into the shipping pens. The boss says, 'I don't believe this! If they had gone straight across the tracks instead of turning left, they would have wound up in the Santa Cruz River.'" When the boys rode back through Amado, the laundress innocently asked, "Did I cause you boys any trouble?" One replied, "Lady, we got some more cattle coming. When we're finished, we'll let you know. Then you can do your wash."

Soon afterwards, Fred started getting itchy feet again and he headed over to Patagonia where he and Dean met up at the Wagon Wheel. The bartender gave them a message from their buddy, Jack, that he had been hired by the Z Bar T Ranch in Portal. He would be at the Gadsden Hotel in Douglas looking for hands and if they wanted a job they should get over there right away. "They already had a foreman hired and this fella, he had the big boots and a big hat and he threw a riata. Well, when we seen (sic) the riata we figured, oh boy, we got problems here."

First thing the foreman says to the boss the following day is, "Mr. Komar, this is the nice kind of young cow that you should get," pointing to an animal that was obviously at least 13 years old. A little later, with the herd standing just a few yards away, he looks at the ground and says, "Mr. Komar, from the looks of these tracks we should be getting on to cattle pretty soon." At this point, Fred asked his friend Jack, "Where did you get this guy from?" "He came from the Faraway Ranch. They highly recommended him," Jack said. Dean shot Fred a look and as they're leaving the corrals the next morning, Dean says, "Hey, look at these tracks," and Fred answers, "Oh, that's the black and white milk cow and from the looks of the tracks she hasn't been milked yet." Time to move on again.

At Wert Bowman's ranch up by Red Rock they had some nice looking horses including a blue roan so gentle nothing could spook him. Old Blue was in Fred's string. At the camp where Fred was tending cattle, there was a broken down fence that needed to be removed. Fred fashioned an apron out of a piece of rawhide to protect Blue's chest, then rode him up to a post and Blue would butt into it and knock it down.

The area was dangerous with a lot of washes among the mesquite that created a problem when it came time to round up the cattle. The only way to get them out was to rope and drag them. "I went after one cow, we crashed through the mesquite, the cow went out of sight down into one of those washes, and I couldn't stop old Blue. Boom, down we went and he fell over on his side."

Fred's left leg was pinned under the horse and he hollered, "Hey Blue, come on wake up." Blue was just lying there with his feet stretched out to the other side of the narrow wash. "He kind of shook his ears like, "Nah, siesta time." While they were lying there trapped, the cow came running back down the wash towards them. Fred realized the wash was a dead end and the cow couldn't get out. "The only way out was over the top of us. I pulled my pistol out and cocked it. I'm gonna have to kill her." Suddenly, Fred hears a shout, "Hey, don't shoot her, we'll rope her." About that time a rope hit the cow and another cowboy passed a rope down for Fred to wrap around the saddle horn and they pulled old Blue upright. Fred and Blue wasted no time getting out of the wash and the cowboys dragged the cow out after them.

"I had a little horse, a company horse that we called Half Pint and he liked to buck." When it came time to change mounts during the roundups, if Half Pint spotted the remuda coming to replace him he would get kind of itchy and start bucking. "I always got him stopped. He was easy to ride. Couldn't buck off a wet saddle blanket."

When winter came and they were cleaning everything out of the mountains Fred noticed a four-year-old steer in with the cows. The foreman said if they thought they could bring him in to go ahead and try. "My partner, Bob, was riding a good-sized horse and I was riding Half Pint. I didn't feel like going for a bronc ride, so Bob threw a loop at him. He caught one horn and that steer throwed (sic) his horn and like to drug him down." Fred knew Half Pint couldn't handle the steer so he didn't even attempt to rope him.

175

Bob's dog could catch cattle by the nose and he started hollering, "Happy. Happy, where the heck are you?" Suddenly, Happy rears up in front of the steer and nabs him and over they go, but the steer kicks him loose. Then the steer runs to the barbed wire fence where the cattle are, crashes through the fence, and stays with the cows on the other side.

"Now here we've got this big steer that's cut himself on the dewlap, so we've got to doctor him and we don't have no chutes(sic). That means we gotta go in there on horseback, put him down and doctor him. Meantime I changed to a bigger horse and we made sure we put a lot of Smear 62, that black worm medicine, on him which showed up good on his white chest. Anyway, they brought in some new horses and took the old horses away. The new ones needed to be broke and I'm getting itchy feet again."

Almost ten years after first setting his itchy feet on Arizona soil Fred ran into Bob Boice at Zary South Saddle Shop in Tucson. Fred was looking for a job and Bob said, "Well, come home with me." This second stint on the Empire lasted for a year and a half. "One day I'd ride with Bob, the next day with his brother, Pancho. By that time everything was slowing down. The Boices sold some of their land and cattle and the ranches got smaller, but we still had a lot of fun."

Itchy feet are the hallmark of the cowboys who perform the day-to-day work on Arizona ranches and Fred was one of the best around. After a stint serving his country in World War II, Fred returned to his adopted state of Arizona to resume the life he loved.

Betty Barr

The Proctor children took "manual training" at the one-room school at Continental on Thursday afternoons to learn woodworking and leather craft. Foreground from left: Charles Proctor forming leather on a shoe last, George and William working on furniture. The traveling teacher brought all the tools and materials each week, in the station wagon seen at right. Circa early 1920s. Photo courtesy George Proctor and the Proctor Museum.

Betty Barr

George Proctor

Madera Canyon and Patagonia

When George Proctor was a little tyke, about five or six years old, his father would press him into service delivering moonshine. His dad, Charles Proctor, had constructed a still completely by hand and used it to produce his highly prized mescal. He would load five-gallon drums filled with the brew on each side of George's little black mare. Smaller, two-gallon containers, would be added on each side of the saddle horn.

With the mare fully loaded, George would take the homemade mescal to designated pickup places scattered all over the Santa Rita Mountains. The rendezvous spots and the location of the still were changed regularly to avoid detection, although George remembers that many of their customers were "government men."

George's family has been in southeastern Arizona for over 100 years. His father, Charles Proctor, was born in Vermont in 1889. Soon afterwards the family moved to Arizona. They settled in the Green Valley area, where Grandfather Proctor operated the stage stop, Tesota, (cat claw in Spanish). Young Charles rode his horse to school at Sahaurita for first and second grades, and then attended Helvetia School for the rest of his elementary education. He was in the first graduating class at Tucson High School in 1910, one of only ten children in the class.

One of Grandfather Proctor's enterprises was raising sheep and goats. The sheepherder he employed would leave his dog to guard the herd, and when the animal got

179

hungry he would come down to the Proctor home looking for a handout. The dog refused to go back to the herd until they fixed him a meal. When the dog had eaten his fill, Proctor would put the leftovers in a sack. The dog would pick the sack up in his mouth and carry it back to his post, where he would stash it until he got hungry again.

Grandfather Proctor was the longtime manager for Maish and Driscoll, owners of the Canoa Ranch, near Green Valley. The outfit had a government contract to supply cattle to the Indians on the reservation at San Carlos. Proctor was in charge of the supply operation, riding many hard miles to deliver the beef. It was soon obvious that the Indians would need horses to help them manage the herds. Although there was an abundance of wild horses in Arizona at the time, the government standards were strict, and many of the local animals did not meet the criteria.

Maish and Driscoll sent Proctor down to a ranch near Hermosillo, Mexico, to purchase quality horseflesh. He then drove the horses all the way back across the border and up north past Safford to the San Carlos Reservation. One story Grandpa told was that during the rainy season he was back at the ranch when two horses showed up. He immediately recognized them as two of the Mexican horses that he had delivered to San Carlos not long before. Grandpa fed them for a few days and then they disappeared. He was sure they had been stolen, but the next time he went to Mexico on a horse buying expedition, there were the same two horses. The "homing pigeons" had retraced their steps all the way from San Carlos to Hermosillo. The Mexican rancher said, "Proctor, take them, you paid for them," but Grandpa refused the offer. He figured if they liked their home that much, they should be allowed to stay there.

After George's father, Charles, graduated from Tucson High, he married Ynez Redondo and in 1918 the young couple set up housekeeping at a little homestead in Madera Canyon. They had to do whatever it took to feed their fast growing family of what would soon become seven children, five boys and two girls. Charles got a job with the state highway department, helping to construct the roads from Tucson to Nogales. He was paid 50 cents an hour for a six-day a week job.

George W. P. Hunt, the first governor of the new state of Arizona, wielded a lot of power at that time. Soon word came down from the capital in Phoenix that everyone on the payroll should be registered as a Democrat. The stated deadline to get on the list was 30 days. When the time arrived, Proctor was still registered as a Republican. He suddenly found himself unemployed and soon returned to moonshining to make ends meet. Although he spent most of his life brewing the libation for the pleasure of others, he never indulged in spirits of any kind himself. According to his son, George, he never even smoked tobacco.

George Proctor remembers that his mother, Ynez, was a creative cook, and put delicious meals on the table, despite their meager supplies. She would throw tortillas over her arm and stretch them out to make them really thin and delicate, or would form them a different way to make gorditas, fat tortillas. She made homemade cheese by putting the curds in cheesecloth, adding weight to it and squeezing out the whey. There was always an ample supply of beans and potatoes, and homemade jerky was a mainstay in their diet. Ynez was also adept at making all kinds of meals out of rice, including soups and a delicious rice pudding that her son George remembers fondly.

When their father would be gone for long periods looking for work, groceries would be in short supply. The children would catch a big gobbler and their mom would boil him up in a five-gallon pot, adding lots of spices. The resulting stew would be a delicious treat for many days. During really hard times, they would have to resort to poaching a deer just to have enough food to put on the table.

When George and his siblings were old enough to go to school, they walked a mile and a half from the homestead in Madera Canyon to catch the school bus for the 13-mile ride to the one-room school at Continental. The boys looked forward to Thursday afternoons, because that was the day that the traveling shop teacher would come to Continental for "manual training." The teacher was named Mr. Basurto, but the students called him Mr. "Basura," Spanish for trash. He would arrive in a station wagon filled with all the tools and materials necessary for the boys to construct their projects. The first few hours of class were a lot of fun as the boys had free rein to create all kinds of woodworking and leather projects. The final hour of the class was devoted to costing out the price of the materials used in each finished piece.

One of the students, Chico Gonzalez, would invariably ask to be excused to the restroom whenever it came time to do the end-of-the-day bookkeeping. One particular day was quite windy and when Chico left the outhouse to return to class, a sudden gust of wind came up and blew the privy off its blocks. Chico ran back to class shouting, Mr. Basura, (Mr. Trash), my excuse just fell down."

Nothing remains today of the old place in Madera Canyon, but Proctor, a retired Forest Service ranger, has preserved his memories with a huge collection of personal and historically significant artifacts at a small but elegant museum at his home near Patagonia. He gathered the items for display with the help of his sister, Margaret Redondo. After erecting a steel frame building on the property, he and his wife, Fran, completely paneled the walls and ceiling in wood, creating a beautiful backdrop for his extensive collection. The project was completed in March of 2001. George, who carries a wealth of information in his head, is happy to describe to visitors the history and purpose of each and every item on display.

The focal point of his collection is the original still that his father made and used during the prohibition years, along with the 100-year old wood trough where the cooked agave was mashed with a wooden mallet. It was a three-day process to cook the agave, another seven days for fermentation, and two passes through the still before straight alcohol started dripping out into the bottle below.

Everything, including all the tools and equipment, was handmade, with nothing wasted. The bootleggers would patch the cracks in the still with flour paste and later they would break off pieces of the hard flour and eat it. If they didn't have enough kegs, they would make a large bota out of cowhide and use that. They got bottles wherever they could find them and used a cork shrinker. The shrunken cork would be fitted into the opening and then would swell up to fit tightly.

The collection runs the gamut from western tack to pioneer household items and includes Indian arrowheads, metates and grinding stones as well as weapons from South America and World War II, where George was wounded in the South Pacific. (All of his brothers also served their country in that war). There is even an engraved silver bit that belonged to Teddy Roosevelt when he hunted bear in the Kaibab, near the Grand Canyon. George obtained the bit with the help of his commanding officer, Archibald Roosevelt, a distant relative of the president.

Rafael Quiroz

Sonora to Sonoita

Rafael Quiroz, foreman of the Crown C Ranch near Sonoita, is a man born to the saddle. Growing up in Mexico, where there were always horses around, Rafael would watch the cowboys break them. He says he was too young to imagine anything bad could happen to him, so he just got on and learned how to do it by himself. Judging by the number of people who call upon him to find them a perfect horse, his methods paid off.

Rafael grew up in the small Sonoran farming town of Sadic, where a mission founded by Father Kino still stands. The tiny town consisted of adobe houses on dirt roads and the family made a meager living buying and selling a few cattle and raising corn, potatoes, beans and cotton. As many others before him, the young Rafael came north looking for a better life. After a few years working in the Flagstaff area he went back to Mexico, got his papers in order, and in 1979 returned to the States with his wife. He was hired at the Crown C, then owned by Blake and Jane Carrington, to work under ranch foreman, Dick Jimenez, and has been at the ranch ever since. He is now the foreman himself.

Towards the end of September in the mid-1980s, Jimenez and Quiroz were out gathering cattle. There was not a cloud overhead as they brought the cattle up over the pass, although they could see black clouds and rain off in the distance in the direction of Fort Huachuca. Suddenly lightning struck and the next thing Rafael knew, he was on the ground, looking up at an ambulance. He had no idea what had hit him, and to this day cannot recall the details of the accident.

Rob Lackey, who was living at the ranch and later became a foreman there, had witnessed the incident and called for help. Lackey later told Rafael that both of the riders and horses went down when the strike occurred. Dick's horse was killed on the spot and he was unconscious and not breathing when Lackey reached his side. According to Dick's daughter, Mercy Jimenez Sumner, the wire strand in his hat-band was melted, his belt buckle was damaged where the strike hit him and he had marks on his behind where the metal rivets of the saddle burned his skin. Even his sideburns were scorched. Lackey administered CPR until the ambulance arrived to transport Jimenez to Holy Cross Hospital in Nogales. From there he was transferred to Tucson Medical Center where he spent about a week. He permanently lost the hearing in one ear.

Quiroz had been riding a good working cow horse when the lightning struck. The horse survived the strike but was never the same again. He became so spooky that he eventually had to be sold. Quiroz suffered from dizziness and ringing in the ears and wasn't able to return to work for ten to 14 days afterwards.

Despite this hair-raising event, Quiroz says he has not had very many bad horse wrecks and except for getting bucked off once in a while has suffered no serious injuries. However, he does admit to broken ribs when a horse slipped one day on a hill and fell on him while he was rounding up cattle. His most serious injury occurred when the crew was trying to put cattle in the corral. A bull came out and pushed him up against the panels and he was hurt badly enough to require a trip to the hospital. To his way of thinking, this is all part of a day's work.

He has spent a lifetime buying, training and selling horses that he brings up from Mexico, many on special order for customers looking for a good working cow horse or a gentle one for the kids. He goes back to his hometown and travels from ranch to ranch to find the ones he wants. He brings them up to the border where they are quarantined and checked for disease and then on to Sonoita where he rides them for a week or two to settle them down before turning them over to their new owners.

Quiroz' early training is all Mexican style, which translates to doing everything manually. As he explains: the difference from the American way is that in Mexico everyone is poor. There are few corrals, no loading chutes or fancy equipment of any kind. The cowboys go out to round up the cattle and have to get it all done in one day because there are no holding pens to corral the cattle while the branding and shots are being handled. If the cattle get loose they are long gone and have to be rounded up again the next day.

The vaqueros still make their reatas by hand, gather cattle in the mountains, stay overnight and eat around a campfire. They do not carry food or jerky with them - only what they need to round up the cattle. They kill a cow out on the range and the camp cook makes the fire and cooks the fresh meat every night. Because of the lack of good equipment, the Mexican vaquero relies heavily on his horse. A good horse to a vaquero is like a pot full of gold to city folk.

Rafael Quiroz is truly a cowboy of the old school and has shared much of his vaquero heritage with his gringo friends over the years. As his neighbor and long-time friend Bruce Andre sums it up, "Rafael is a good cowman and a great one to have on a roundup. Let's face it, the Mexican vaquero has been here a lot longer than we have!"

Ronnie Pyeatt displays his roping skills at the Sonoita Fairgrounds in 1954.
Photo courtesy Pyeatt family

Ronnie Pyeatt

Pyeatt Ranch

"All I ever really wanted to do was rope." Ronnie Pyeatt's eyes take on a far-away look as his mind casts back over the years. "I was about 18 and had won the first go round in calf roping at the Benson Rodeo. I had a good calf the next day and was looking forward to roping him. There was a railroad track running past the arena," his hands describe an arc in the air. "The calf loped out, I roped him and just as I stood in the saddle, the engineer blew the whistle. I was riding a good little horse, but it scared him and he jumped sideways and dropped my head in the ground. All I could think of was tying that calf, but I was half addled and it took forever to get him tied and get back on the horse."

The years roll away and the smell of the sweat and dust and the feel of the hard packed arena against the cowboy's face become a reality as his words bring the past to life. "I'll never forget the sound of Del Haverty laughing as he yelled to me, 'Well, your ground work's getting better!'"

Pyeatt's family homesteaded near the West Gate entrance to Fort Huachuca. His dad Buster is a legend in these parts. Ronnie was born at the base hospital and grew up on the family's ranch where riding and roping were the best part of life. Building fences and working on windmills was where the romance of the Wild West ended and a herd of milk cows could really cramp a kid's style.

No matter what you were doing, you had to be home in time for milking. The family had a Holstein that gave a lot more milk than the Herefords. They would feed her milk to the hogs and dogies and still have pans of milk covered with gunnysacks in the desert cooler. When the cream came to the top it would be skimmed off and the milk underneath would be blue with a few specks of cream floating on top. Homogenized milk was like a taste of heaven compared to that! There was always a flour sack full of clabber, or curds, hanging on the stove that would be used to make cheese.

One time his mom had set a bunch of eggs and only one hatched out of about 20. They called the chick "Lucky" and she stayed around the ranch and became a family pet. One afternoon, when Ronnie thought everyone was asleep, he decided to practice his roping. In spite of her name, Lucky had the misfortune to amble by at that moment. He roped her good and she let out a squawk that roused the household.

Ronnie was in big trouble, but he still roped anything and everything that moved and even some things that didn't.

His love of roping came with the territory. His father was also passionate about the sport. A neighbor, Mr. Houston, weaned some cows and turned them loose by the Pyeatt Ranch. When a buyer came along, Houston rounded the heifers into a corral for the man to look them over. The buyer said, "Mr. Houston, these cows seem pretty gentle." Houston replied, "They were raised over by Pyeatts, so they're probably rope-broke." Buster, Buckshot Sorrells and Joe Mapes were all living there at the time and all they did all day was rope Houston's cattle for fun. Sorrels later became a rodeo cham-

Buster Pyeatt with his two boys, Jim and Ronnie at the Tucson Rodeo Grounds in 1939.
Photo courtesy Jim Pyeatt

pion and marched in the parade in New York City when he performed at Madison Square Garden.

The movie, "Red River" with John Wayne, was filmed in Elgin in 1946. The teacher at the Canelo School was dating one of the cameramen and took the class on many "field trips" to the location. The crew dammed up the San Pedro River at Fairbanks and drove the 1,600 head of cattle down the right of way to "swim the Red River." The cattle got gentle from standing around so much and when it came time for the stampede scene, they wouldn't move. Finally the movie crew dug a pit, put a charge of dynamite in, covered it with rocks and drove the steers out there. When they shot it off, the stampede was awesome.

One of the scenes called for Wayne to set up camp in a spot that he wanted to stake out for a ranch. In the script, some Mexican vaqueros rode up and told him the land belonged to their boss. He could only stay there a week. When Wayne protested, the Mexican reached for his gun. Wayne beat him to the draw but his gun just clicked and clicked. After filming was done, Wayne was gassing up at the local filling station when Stone Collie drove up and Wayne laughingly told him, "I forgot to load the damn thing."

"I loved to rope, but the Elgin/Canelo baseball games were great, too," Ronnie remembers fondly. Mal Eason, who owned the Umpire Ranch, was a retired major league baseball player who used to hang out at the Canelo Store. He formed a baseball team of kids and adults and he was the coach. Soon, Stone Collie put a group together in Elgin with

Buster Pyeatt was well known as a horseman as well as a roper. Circa 1940.
Photo courtesy Jim Pyeatt.

Bill Brophy of the Babacomari Ranch as pitcher. The games were played at the picnic area in Canelo and were fierce battles. Bob Hale was on the Elgin team, and being from Boston thought he knew just as much about the game as Eason. He and Mal would start shouting in each other's faces and the fun would begin. Even Ronnie's mother was pressed into service and, "She couldn't catch a towel if you threw it to her." Canelo had won three games in a row but when they went to Elgin's home turf they got beaten. The pang of that defeat broke their hearts.

A prospector named Jim Hogan lived at an old mining claim between Pyeatt's Ranch and Fort Huachuca. Ronnie and the other kids liked to go over there because Hogan could carve slingshots and whistles out of willow sticks for them. He used tin cups and plates and when he was finished eating he'd put the dishes on the floor. His dog, Worthless, would lick everything clean and Hogan would put it back on the shelf. He had an outhouse and used Sears Roebuck catalogs for toilet paper. His two burros loved to eat paper, so Ronnie obligingly fed them pages from the catalog, piece by piece, until his dad noticed what was going on and put an end to the fun.

Mr. Anderson was an old fellow who held a real fascination for the kids – he was a nudist. Ronnie remembers riding along with his dad when Buster suddenly burst out laughing, "Here comes Mr. Anderson." He was wearing a hat and a pair of shoes, and was carrying a shovel. He greeted them saying, "You know, I have to be kinda careful, I could be caught in an embarrassing predicament here."

There were dances every weekend in the San Rafael Valley or in Huachuca City, where Wild Horse Shorty and his wife played at Will and Rosa's Halfway House, or at the Elgin Club. Ronnie would try to sleep in the back of the car while his folks danced, but there were so many fights in the parking lot he would just lie there and pray for the dance to be over so he could go home. He would get carsick and Grandma didn't make matters any better by dipping Garrett's snuff. It came in a big jar or little tin cans and every so often they had to stop and pull up some grass roots so that she could make a kind of burl, dip it into her snuff can and put it back in her mouth. Pioneer women were tough.

Betty Barr

James Henry and Mary Ollie Kelly Pyeatt. Circa 1887.
Photo courtesy Jim Pyeatt

Pyeatt family

Pyeatt Ranch

Earthquakes keep popping up in the Pyeatt family's history. A king-sized trembler in 1887 rocked southeastern Arizona a few short days after Henry and Mary Pyeatt were married, in a ceremony conducted at what is now the ghost town of Charlestown. Nine years later, Buster, the youngest of the couple's nine children, was born on April 18, 1906, the same day the famous earthquake devastated San Francisco.

While not as well known, the Arizona quake was more than impressive to those who lived through it. Henry Pyeatt told a newsman that he had gone to the general store in Palominas that day, leaving his new bride home alone at their nearby ranch.

He was swapping stories with three local cowboys on the front porch of the store, when the men were brought abruptly to their feet by the sound of a distant rumbling, closely followed by chunks of plaster falling off the storefront and cracks opening up in the street. In the ensuing confusion, they all ran out into the plaza and then dashed back to the store, fearing they were either going to be crushed by the falling walls or swallowed by the crevasses opening up on the street.

"It was so funny," Pyeatt told a newsman at the time. "We ran like wild calves. Old Cap Kelton didn't run, he just moved away from the adobe wall and said, 'Don't get excited boys. It's nothing but an earthquake.'"

James "Henry" Pyeatt was born in San Saba, Texas in 1861. As a boy, he picked cotton in east Texas, worked as a cowpuncher in the Indian territory of Oklahoma and followed the historic Butterfield Trail into Dodge City, Kansas. An honest man who never looked for trouble, Pyeatt often said of those days, "You can read about what happened in Dodge City in a thousand and one books and stories, and they are nearly all true. But when the shooting started, I started the other way!"

In 1882, at the age of 21, Henry hired on as a cowboy for a company moving 1,000 head of Texas longhorns to Arizona; his sole possessions a horse and a saddle. A cowboy at heart, he had no interest in searching for gold or silver, a quest that consumed many new arrivals to the territory, and he soon found work at B. A. Packard's famed Turkey Track Cattle Company east of Douglas. The ranch was later owned by John Slaughter, a famous Indian fighter and sheriff of Cochise County. After Slaughter's death in 1922, the historic ranch was restored and is now open to the public as the Slaughter Ranch Museum.

In a 1939 issue of the Western Livestock Journal, Pyeatt's old Texas friend, James Powell, talked about cowboying alongside Pyeatt. "I came out with a trail herd of 2,200 cattle. Our outfit adjoined the Slaughter Ranch (where his buddy Pyeatt had located).

"When a cattle buyer came along he usually had his saddlebags packed full of gold and silver. He'd throw (them) by the chuckwagon and go out to look over the cattle. Sometimes it was several days before we could round up all the stock he wanted. All that time a fortune in hard money lay in those saddlebags, but nobody thought anything about it. When the buyer had the cattle, he dug into his saddlebags and got out enough double eagles and silver to pay for his purchase. That was the frontier way of doing business."

Upon arriving in Arizona territory, Pyeatt soon realized that the "bad hombres" of those days, the gamblers, gold seekers and gun-slinging desperados, usually claimed to be Texans, giving that state a bad reputation. Hoping to distance himself from a questionable background, Pyeatt let it be known that he had been born in Missouri. When in later years he admitted to his Texas origins, many old-timers could not be convinced that he didn't hail from Missouri.

Although a peace-loving man, Pyeatt was involved in two campaigns against Geronimo. Never one to glamorize his exploits, Pyeatt recounted the tale realistically: "The group was fired more by zeal to capture the fast-fleeing Indian outlaws than by prudence or skill. With all dispatch and openness, they sallied forth in one body, down through the Guadalupe Valley to the Ajo Mountains and into Old Mexico. It was springtime, which made it easier to keep to the trail for three days and nights."

On the third day they gave up the chase. "It is a good thing we had sense enough to do that," Pyeatt recalled, "for if we had stayed, the Indians would have killed us all. We were just crazy kids strung out along the trail. It's a wonder they didn't ambush us. We camped one night in a big canyon, right out in the open (and) built as big fires as we could. The next morning we climbed on up the mountain, and there on a rimrock was where Geronimo and his braves had camped. They had looked right down on us and probably laughed all that time. We counted the remains of eleven campfires on the ridge." To taunt them, the Indians had left an old black satin coat buttoned around a scrub oak bush near the campfire.

In the late 1880s Henry bought the A Triangle and XH Bar ranches at Palominas, along the riparian area of the San Pedro River. After selling the ranches to Colonel William Greene in 1899, he bought the MX Ranch from a man by the improbable name of Hugo Igo, on the far northwest end of the Huachuca Mountains. Pyeatt purchased 75 mares in addition to the cattle that came with the MX brand. Igo also had quarters on the property that he used as a guest ranch and convalescent home for miners recovering from "Black Lung" disease.

The ranch was established around a group of four large springs and boasted a beautiful natural pond. Igo had planted an orchard of over a thousand trees that flourished with the help of the constant supply of spring water. His produce was highly prized all over the state and one account tells of Igo arriving in Prescott with two wagons overflowing with apples for sale.

Henry Pyeatt built this home in 1917. It features dormer windows in the roof and a porch on all four sides. The same type of construction was used in the officer's quarters at Fort Huachuca, that was built in the early 1900s.
Photos courtesy Jim Pyeatt

The Pyeatt homestead, near the West Gate of Fort Huachuca, boasted four springs and a lush pond.

Pyeatt continued to cultivate the orchard until the early 1920s when the McFadden Mining Company started operations nearby, depleting the ground water. The trees began to die and when Pyeatt asked McFadden to recycle the water and pipe it back to the orchard, they refused. He sued to stop their operations, but by the time he won the case, in 1926, it was too late to save the trees.

Henry Pyeatt with his prized Hereford, Pug, the cow with a penchant for apricots. Henry fenced her out of the yard to protect his tree, but one morning he returned home to find the tree smashed and all the fruit devoured. Pug had managed to get in the yard and according to Henry, "The only way she could have done that much damage was to climb up on the porch and jump into the middle of it." Circa 1930.
Photo courtesy Jim Pyeatt

In 1907, eight of Henry Pyeatt's finest saddle horses were stolen and driven into Mexico. According to John Yoas, a neighboring rancher who chased the thieves across the border, his attempt to negotiate with Mexican officials to follow the robbers "to the end of the road," was refused. He returned home without Pyeatt's horses, said to be the best of his herd. According to accounts at the Pimeria Alto Historical Society, "Yoas said...he is pretty certain that one of the thieves was Billy Stiles, all-around bad man and Arizona bandit... Yoas would give anything to get within a few hundred yards of him...Stiles would take great pleasure in exchanging compliments with Yoas. Both men are dead shots..."

Of all the horses that were stolen, the only one that Pyeatt got back was "Yellow Willie." It just so happened that a cousin of Pyeatt's, Roland Curry, was in Douglas one day, and saw someone riding Yellow Willie down the street. He reported the sighting to the sheriff and Yellow Willie was returned to Pyeatt, the only one of the stolen horses that was ever seen again.

By 1913, Pyeatt had developed a large, quality herd. That year he sold 1,200 head of cows, calves, bulls and two-, three-, and four-year-old steers to a Texan he had known from the old Dodge City days. After the orchard died, he turned his full attention to the cattle business and improved the herd by bringing in Durham and quality Herefords to achieve uniform bone structure and color.

In spite of his commitment to ranching, Pyeatt dabbled briefly in mining. Two prospectors had been poking around in the hills near the ranch and came to him with a proposition. If he would stake them with 400 canvass sacks and haul the ore from the ranch to the Huachuca siding for shipment to Bisbee, they would do all the other work. Pyeatt agreed, and when their first shipment was complete, they were $7.50 short of repaying his investment. Pyeatt quit mining then and there. "It takes a miner to mine," he often said, "I'll stick to cattle."

When Henry passed away in 1942, his son Buster bought the ranch from the estate. He and his wife, Rose Richie, the daughter of a mining engineer from Cananea, Mexico raised their two sons, Ronnie and Jim, at the old family ranch.

Methods changed after the "open range" era of the early days ended, and Buster cut back on the number of cattle the ranch produced and practiced rotation and proper management plans to restore the range to a viable state. The ranch became much smaller when the Fort Huachuca Military Reservation took a large portion of the grazing lands for a bombing range after World War I. More acreage went to the government when the U.S. Forest Service was organized.

Buster Pyeatt added a successful quarter horse breeding program to the business in the 1940s. He bought a seven-month old colt named Snooper from Cicero Martin of Sonoita. After Snooper finished first at the Rillito Race Track in Tucson in 1945, he became a valuable stud horse. Rose Fulton, of the Dragoon Ranch, was racing Settle Up, the younger brother of Snooper. Although her colt was doing well on the track, he didn't generate as much stud business as Snooper. To prove once and for all who had the best stallion, the Fultons challenged the Pyeatts to a race in 1949. In a hotly contested effort, Snooper passed Settle Up to cross the finish line in first place.

The ranch now operates under the guidance of James "Jim" Pyeatt, Henry's grandson and namesake. Jim is the third generation to run the ranch as a commercial and registered Hereford cow-calf operation. Jim says that there are still three springs on the property today, although the pond is long gone and one spring is starved for water due to the drought. They now supplement with wells.

The Pyeatt family celebrated its 100th anniversary of ranch life in 1999. Including Jim's children and grandchildren, there have now been five generations of the family continuously living and working on this historic ranch.

Following in the family tradition, Jim's grandson, Manuel Murrietta, has now joined him in the ranch operations. Manuel has inherited his great-grandfather's love of cattle ranching. As Jim Pyeatt puts it, "Manuel is a natural on the ranch. I couldn't run this place without him."

A youthful Alex Gonzales displays his horsemanship at Pryor's Diamond C Ranch in Lyle Canyon, now owned by Rukin Jelks, Jr. Circa 1920s.
Photo courtesy Alex Gonzales.

Alex Gonzales

West Gate

In a manner of speaking, Pancho Villa deserves some of the credit for Alex Gonzales being born in Patagonia. In 1911 Timoteo Gonzales, one of Villa's band of revolutionaries, "went over the hill" and headed into the Arizona wilderness to seek a better life. He found work in the mines around Patagonia and the following year in Nogales he met Maria Chavez, who had recently arrived from Chihuahua. They soon married and Alex was born at the RRR Mine Camp near Patagonia in 1914.

The little family of three lived in a tent and Timoteo would ride off into the mountains every morning to do assessment work for the mine. Miners were required to spend $100 on each Forest Service claim every year and many of them had hundreds of claims up in the hills. Timoteo would be sent to camp out at the claim and he would stay there as long as it took him to complete the work.

When it came time for Alex to go to school, the family moved to the San Rafael Valley where his father worked cattle on Clyde McPherson's ranch and also had a little farm. Their adobe house was located on what is now the Vaca Ranch near the Cottonwood Windmill. One of his earliest memories as a wide-eyed little boy is of watching a mule pulling a grindstone round and round to grind up cane. One of the homesteaders in the valley was a very good farmer in spite of the drought. His sorghum crop was so large that he hired someone to come in with a mule and a mill to prepare the cane for sale.

A few years later his dad had an opportunity to do a little farming in the Canelo area in what is now called West Gate. In a week's time he would only see about 15 cars go by, but there were always many little buckboards and horse drawn wagons. The Gonzales' garden was close to the road and all the passersby knew Timeteo. They would tie their horses or team up to the fence, crawl through, feast on the watermelons and cantaloupe and then ride off. In spite of this friendly pilfering, there was usually enough of a cash crop for market.

Timoteo dry-farmed the land. He would plow the ground in January and February, put the corn in on the 5th and 6th of May, and if it didn't rain in a month there was no crop. Fort Huachuca operated a dairy at that time with about 50 head of milk cows. Timoteo's garden provided the corn for their feed. There was no irrigation, so he planted beans right after the first rain and, if it continued raining, he would get a crop in six weeks. Often he would harvest two tons of pintos, but at two cents per pound it took a lot of beans to put any food on their table.

Timoteo arranged for credit at the country store in White City, which was later known as Fry, and finally became Sierra Vista. The family was able to buy flour, coffee and supplies throughout the year and as soon as it got cold enough to butcher, he would slaughter a beef and take the meat down to the store to settle up for the groceries. This is the way most of the families in the area survived in those days.

The Army base used wood fuel and every spring and winter they would let bids for woodcutting. The wood would be cut with axes, brought down to the road, loaded on trucks or burros and transported onto the base to use in the barracks' wood heaters. The oak would be clear-cut all the way from West Gate, through the base as far as Carr Canyon and Miller Canyon.

The base also operated its own bakery. When Alex was working a construction job in Huachuca City, there was no commuting so the guys were camping out at the job site. One morning the sergeant came by and asked if they would like any food from the commissary. They handed him 50 cents and told him to bring back some bread. The sergeant said, "You want all this in bread?" and they said, "Sure." He came back with 24 freshly baked loaves. The locals would also go to the base where a haircut could be had for 35 cents and for another 50 cents you could purchase a great beefsteak.

In 1928 the family moved to the Rodgers Ranch (now the Whitney Ranch in Canelo). Mr. Rodgers was the first postmaster there, operating out of a tent on the property. Rodgers was also the first Forest Ranger for the District and he was responsible for the entire Coronado Forest including the Huachucas, the Santa Ritas, the Whetstones and the Patagonias. He had a little black horse and twice a year he rode the entire forest to make a report on the conditions.

During the summer, he was given one helper in case of fire. Alex joined the Forest Service in 1936 and became a fireguard. The service provided him with an old Chevy pickup to use. When the Second World War came along Alex joined up and he says when he returned four years later, they were still using the same truck. After ten years they finally bought him a new one.

The service was spread pretty thin, so when a fire broke out Alex would take off and try to pick up volunteers on the way wherever he could find them. In 1948 they acquired a field phone that was housed in a little wooden box. Alex would throw a wire over a tree, hook it onto the box and hope to connect with someone. Twice a month he would saddle his horse and load a pack mule with a two-week supply of batteries for the radio to make his rounds. To save battery power the lookout stationed at the top of Miller Peak only turned the radio on every half-hour, during emergencies Alex used a Navy signal glass to get the lookout's attention. He would aim it at the sun and direct the beam toward the window of the lookout tower as a signal to turn on the radio.

Alex's teacher at the Canelo one-room school was Mrs. Oliver, who drove over from Fort Huachuca each day in an old jalopy. He had already finished the 5th grade in San Rafael so he started in 6th grade at the beginning of the year. After about a week, Mrs. Oliver asked him if he would like to try 7th grade. There was one other boy already in 7th and Alex jumped at the chance to join him. A few more weeks went by and she let them go into 8th. In this unorthodox fashion, he zipped through three grades in one school year.

The big fun on weekends was for the kids to saddle up and ride cross-country about ten miles to Elgin for the dances. In the winter it would be bitter cold, but they would just grab a coat and take off on their horses. Coming home, it would get so darn cold that by the time they got to the Research Ranch area they would be half frozen. They would look around for a yucca that was all dead in the middle. One of the kids could always be counted on to have a pack of matches, and they would set it on fire to warm themselves up. When the fire burned out, they would ride on a few more miles, find another yucca and do the same thing all over again.

Not all of Alex's adventures happened when he was a kid. Just a few years ago, he was driving past the Cienega near Canelo when he heard a mother cow bawling and stopped to investigate. Her calf had gotten trapped in the creek and was gasping for breath and sinking in deep water. Alex emptied his pockets, jumped into the pool, grabbed the calf around its belly with both arms and managed to drag him up onto the bank. He took hold of the leg and put pressure on it to see if it would straighten out and it did, so he cupped his hands around the calf's mouth and nose and started breathing into him. After a while he felt a little activity on the chest and turned it around and then it started kicking. The calf wobbled over to the mother but she was evidently suspicious of the human smell on him. She sniffed around him a little while before she let him get some food.

Alex retired from the Forest Service in 1975 but he's not one to sit around on the front porch watching the world go by. His reputation as a master craftsman of beautiful furniture that he builds from mesquite, oak, and juniper and other woods, is

Alex strikes a pose on his fancy car. Circa 1920s.
Photo courtesy Alex Gonzales.

well known. People are constantly stopping by with wonderful pieces of wood that he transforms into tables, lamps, shelves and hiking staffs. His front yard is over-flowing with works in progress and his creations have found homes all over the country and as far away as Boston where his daughter, Maria, lives and works as an architect.

His wife, Elizabeth, came to this country as an English nanny for the Porter family when they had the Singing Valley Ranch. The couple is an integral part of the West Gate community. They organize the annual Canelo family picnic, which is attended by hundreds of present and past residents, and were voted "Couple of the Year" by the Sonoita-Elgin Chamber of Commerce in 1996.

Beth Smith Aycock, "Dude Wrangler," at the Kenyon
Ranch in the 1940s.
Photo courtesy Beth Aycock.

Beth Aycock

Frontier cattlewoman

Watching the tall, slim and elegant Beth Smith Aycock "unfold," as she puts it, out of the car, the term frontier cattlewoman does not immediately spring to mind. Nevertheless, with family roots stretching across southern Arizona ranches from Tucson to Tombstone, Patagonia, Sonoita and Elgin, Beth epitomizes the true spirit of the pioneer west.

Her mother, Nell Choate, was born in Tombstone while the family was enroute to the Chiricahuas to make a new home for themselves. The Choate family had just been evicted from the Babacomari Ranch near Elgin. The Spanish Land Grant was unfenced range at the time and the Choates had built one of the original adobe houses there. After the Civil War, Dr. E. B. Perrin purchased rights to the grant and the Choates, along with several other squatter families, had been forced to leave their homes.

Beth's father was Red Howell, a well-known cowman of the period, who managed such ranches as the Crown C in Sonoita and the A-7, now known as the Bellota Ranch, on the San Pedro River near Vail.

As the only girl in a family of three brothers and 18 male cousins, Beth was destined to become a valued "top hand." When she married Sam Smith in the early 1940s their first job was working as wranglers at the prestigious "blue stocking" Kenyon Ranch near Tubac. The resort was famous throughout the country as a dude ranch. Wealthy clients made reservations years in advance for the privilege of experiencing the colorful "Wild West" in luxurious surroundings. Sam worked with the older riders, Al Donau took out the young people, and Beth taught riding lessons to the children.

According to Beth, she has only been bucked off twice in her life and the most memorable occasion occurred at Kenyon Ranch when Donau wanted to show off to a pretty girl. There was a horse named High Pockets in the string, which could be counted on to buck if you spurred him in the flank, but Beth knew she could ride him. Al's plan was for Beth to kick him up and then he would gallop to her rescue in front of the admiring audience. Al was slightly distracted by the adoring young lady and when Beth energetically acted her part she was bucked off a little earlier than planned. Donau belatedly arrived for the rescue and his horse ran right over her - not exactly the grand finale they had envisioned.

After several years at Kenyon, the young couple moved to the A-7 Ranch to work for her father, Red Howell. The road to the ranch house was completely washed out so the last eight miles had to be traveled on horseback. When Beth's first baby was born they managed to get to St. Mary's Hospital in Tucson in their borrowed Model A Ford in time for the delivery. She and the baby spent eleven days there. When it came time to return to the ranch, Beth had to ride the last eight miles to the house on horseback, with the newborn baby tucked between her and the saddle horn.

Then the well went dry. Sam found a tank at a working windmill up the canyon. He rigged up his mule with a barrel strapped to two stout poles, planning to drag a supply of water back to the ranch. By the time that ornery old mule snaked the barrel down the rocky canyon there were only a few inches of the precious liquid left. Every ounce was like pure gold and was hoarded religiously.

First it was warmed on the stove to bathe the baby. The residue was then used to sterilize the bottles and the remainder was again recycled to wash the dishes and clothes. Whatever was left was utilized to mop the kitchen floor. The last few drops went to quench the thirst of the two saplings they were trying to get started by the front door. This was their creative answer to water conservation.

The ceilings of the old house were constructed of ocotillo stalks and visiting cowboys warned her that they were the preferred nesting spots of scorpions. The stories went that scorpion bites could be fatal to small children, so the new mother spent several sleepless nights aiming a flashlight on the ceiling to guard against this danger. She finally solved the problem by rigging up a screen and putting pails of water under all four legs of the crib, figuring that the scorpions would drown before reaching her baby.

In the late 1940s, Beth and Sam came to the Patagonia area where he was employed by the United States Forest Service. They lived on Sonoita Creek where Beth took care of the registered cattle belonging to Mr. Barnett, who was foreman at the Empire Ranch. For this she was paid $15 a month and given free rent.

The couple spent many years at Rancho del Lago, near the Saguaro National Monument East, and then at a ranch near Canelo. When Sam died in 1977, Beth ran 200 head of cattle, worked part-time at Elgin School and also was the manager at the Sonoita Fairgrounds, earning the princely salary of $3,000 per year. When she arranged for the sale and shipment of horses to Hawaii, she met a dashing polo player, Bill Aycock, who would become her second husband.

Beth peppers her reminiscences with humorous stories and jokes and a twinkle in her eye, evocative of the style of the legendary John Hance who enthralled visitors to the Grand Canyon with tales of the old time cowboys. She has written the first book of a planned trilogy based on frontier stories passed down through her family. *Round Up a Whirlwind* chronicles the exciting period between 1830 and 1870 when the west was being settled by hardworking, hard riding men and women. Beth says that her book proves the old saying, "The West is hell on horses and women." Anyone who meets her in person would take exception to that conclusion.

A rusty Babacomari Ranch sign located on the far west boundary of their range, is a magnet for target shooters. (A secondary spelling of Babocomari is also correct.)
Barr photo.

Brophy, Bidegain and Babacomari

Elgin

It's 27 miles long, three miles wide and a river runs through it. The Babacomari, both the ranch and the river, derives its name from an Indian word whose meaning remains obscured in the mists of time. The river rises up in Elgin and meanders its way through the ridges and draws to the ghost town of Fairbanks where it empties into the San Pedro River, ultimately joining up with the Colorado as it makes its way to the Gulf. The headquarters of the ranch lies in the exact center of this long stretch of land where a spring combines with the river itself to form a beautiful pond.

The fertile banks of the year-round river have sustained life for centuries. Fray Marcos de Niza wrote of receiving a warm welcome from the Upper Pimas who occupied the Babacomari Village site when the explorer discovered it in 1539 and claimed it for the King of Spain. Three hundred years later, Don Ignacio Elias purchased 130,000 usable acres from the Mexican government and called it San Ignacio del Babacomari. When family members were massacred by Apache war parties, the survivors were forced to flee back to Mexico. After the Civil War, Dr. E. B. Perrin purchased the rights to the land grant from the Elias heirs. Frank Cullen Brophy purchased the land in 1935 making the Brophy family the third owner in the 400 years since the early explorers passed through this region.

Pete Bidegain arrived at the Babacomari in June of 1961, hired by Frank Brophy to manage his Hereford cow/calf operation. At that time the two biggest problems faced by ranchers in the area were screwworm and pinkeye. Bidegain's crew would ride the range every day searching the brush for afflicted cattle. They constructed makeshift medicine kits by cutting the tops off an old pair of boots, stitching them together at the narrow end to make a pouch and then attaching a sort of leather strap at the top to tie them onto the saddle. This ingenious invention was just the right size for a one-day's supply of medicine.

Peter Bidegain convinces a calf to turn around and mother-up with the rest of the herd that has already moved up the hill. This "knot-headed calf got confused and ran the wrong way," Pete explains. Taken at the Babacomari, circa 1960.
McChesney photo, courtesy Peter Bidegain.

They ran about 800 cows each year and Brophy always made sure there was an adequate crew to help with all the extra work a cow/calf operation entails. To the west of the manager's quarters, Aurelio and Victoria Duran lived in an adobe house built in the 1880s by the Choate family who squatted there after the Apaches had been removed from the area. Duran handled the well and other maintenance and Victoria cooked for the cowboys. Out in the back was the bunkhouse where Pedro Monteverde and Ventura and about ten or 15 other Mexican cowboys from Magdelena and Hermosillo stayed. They had green cards to work in the U.S. legally and sent money back to support their families in Mexico.

Frank Fisher was a gringo who was always playing pranks on everyone. He would put the kids' saddles on backwards claiming that they were heading east that day and they would retaliate by throwing a lizard - he was deathly afraid of them - through the bathroom window when he was taking a shower. Monday mornings Mrs. Bidegain cautioned the children to steer clear of the driveway between their house and Aurelio's because when Frank returned from a weekend of drinking in town he would speed through the gates, barely missing the posts on either side. Pete always gave him part of Monday off to recover from the weekend saying, "He was our best hand and worked harder than any of the others."

Huge sacaton flats flourish down near the river and once the grass gets high and woody the cattle won't touch it. Mr. Brophy wanted different areas of it burned every five or six years. Burning was done just before rainy season - it would come right back up and the cattle would eat the tender green shoots. The cowboys would take burlap feed bags, leave a string on them, wrap them in baling wire and soak them in diesel all night. Other burlap bags were soaked in water and used as flappers to put the fire out later.

The next day Bidegain's boys, Peter and Todd, would get to drag the bags out to the flats and ignite them. The fires would roar up the canyons toward Fort Huachuca and then the general would call and say, "Mr. Bidegain, you're making us a little nervous over here." It sometimes got a little tricky, according to Bidegain, but they never did have a fire get away from them. Peter and Todd credit this early experience with steering them to their future careers. Both are firemen, Todd in Tucson and Peter at Ft. Huachuca.

House calls are a rarity today, but in the not so distant past they often meant the difference between life and death for both man and beast. Pete was riding a ridge at the top of a riverbank when his horse suddenly fell and plunged down an embankment. Pete hurt his chest and was feeling poorly, so after a few days he went to Patagonia to see Dr. Mock, who gave him a shot for pain and sent him home. That evening he passed out cold, and when they called for Dr. Mock he drove the 32 miles out to the ranch in 20 minutes flat. "He always did drive like a maniac," Bidegain laughs. He rigged up an IV, which Mrs. Bidegain and Todd held out the window of Mock's station wagon all the way to St. Joseph's Hospital in Tucson. When the emergency room doctor came out to meet the man who had saved Bidegain's life, Dr. Mock was already halfway back to Patagonia.

Livestock got the same kind of TLC from Dr. Jim "Doc" Pickrell. Cows never need a Caesarean at a convenient time of day and this particular cow was no exception. At close to midnight in the middle of a tremendous rainstorm the cow got in trouble. Doc was at a fancy party in Nogales, but he got to the Babacomari about 1 a.m. and proceeded to perform a C-section out in the corral in the mud and pouring rain. He and his date were in formal attire, his tuxedo was covered with mud and blood, but cow and calf survived. "It was a flawless performance," according to Bidegain.

"Frank Brophy was quite a guy," Bidegain says. "People said I wouldn't last ten days with him and I stayed 14 years. Wouldn't have left then, except I got sick." Brophy was an Irishman whose family had come to the U.S. via Canada and the goldfields of California in the mid-1800s. He was born in Bisbee in 1894 and was politely invited to leave several prestigious schools for "rowdiness" before finally receiving a degree from Yale. He made money in banking, cattle, real estate and Wall Street, wrote for Arizona Highways and always said he wanted to be a contributor to Playboy Magazine.

He spent weekends and summers at the Babacomari, driving down from Phoenix in his Mercedes, which he had fitted out with a steel plate underneath so he could ride the range in comfort. Bidegain says "I always offered to drive him in my pickup, but he would just tell me to jump in the Mercedes and off we'd go, clanking and bumping over rocks and ruts." One day in the midst of a summer monsoon, one of the kids spotted Mr. Brophy trudging up the driveway on foot. Seems the Mercedes flooded out in the bottom of the dip leading into the ranch. At the end of the storm, all that could be seen of the car was the roof.

Brophy raised Thoroughbred racehorses and always rode English, even when he helped separate the cows. Round-ups were a joint effort with all the neighbors, Dick Jimenez, Frank Figueroa, Lyncho Leon, Clay Howell and Bill Piper among others, helping each other round-robin style. They would start at one ranch and make the circuit, timing it so they would hit the Babacomari for lunch - Victoria's shredded beef and home-made tortillas were legendary.

Bally Brophy, the shipping corrals named in honor of the owner's Irish heritage, were near the railroad tracks that ran along the river. The train would stop at the corrals and the cattle would be loaded up for their brief ride to Sonoita where they would continue their journey by truck.

Bidegain remembers, "Mr. Brophy was very considerate of people." He let a Mexican family live in an old house near the shipping corrals for free and put a trailer on the west end for his horse trainer, Mac McMillan, when he got on in years. Bidegain's son, Todd, concurs, "We had one of the better operations. Dad had a decent wage and we got our gasoline, all our groceries and the meat for free. The Brophy family took care of us."

Portrait of Frank C. Brophy with his favorite stallion hangs above the fireplace in the original adobe house on the ranch. Brophy took the palomino to the Olympics with the U.S. Calvary, but the horse broke his leg while unloading from the trailer and had to be put down before he had a chance to compete.
Betty Barr photo

Enrique piles the third 70-kilo bundle of bear grass on his sturdy burro before leading him down to the pickup spot where his load will be trucked to a factory in Agua Prieta for processing. Barr photo.

Betty Barr

The beargrass cutters

Sonora to Sonoita

A towering silhouette looming on the horizon slowly takes shape as it nears the pickup spot. The image sharpens, revealing a trio of burros laden with bundles of beargrass cut by part of the crew working just over the hill. At the pickup spot, Hector Manuel Torres uses a short-handled scythe to free the cut leaves of beargrass from the center of the plants he has been working on. A truck, scheduled to arrive from Agua Prieta the following day, will weigh and load the bundles of grass for the twice-weekly trip across the border to the Fibrias y Mangos (Fibers and Handles) Factory.

The beargrass cutters, Jesus, Miguel, Julio and Alvaro, represent a dying breed in a dying industry. They make a continuous circuit across the ranchlands of Arizona and New Mexico, returning to each ranch about every three years to harvest the grass. They pay the rancher a minimal fee to come onto his property, where they camp out with their donkeys and a dog and stay until all the full-grown grass is harvested.

At each ranch, the men select a sheltered spot to pitch their tents. This is not communal living; each of the five men has his own cooking gear and fixes his meals at his own tent area at the end of the workday. One of the cutters has rigged up an old water barrel as a makeshift cook-stove while others cook over an open fire.

Crockery and well-used pots and pans eliminate the need for paper products and help keep the camp neat, tidy and free of trash.

The work crew camps out at each ranch they visit. Some have rigged up propane heaters to combat temperatures in the high teens during cold weather. Despite the primitive conditions, the camp is neat and tidy.
Barr photo.

To combat freezing nighttime temperatures during the cooler months of the year, some of the men have rigged up propane heaters to supplement their bedrolls and blankets. Water barrels are trucked in so the workers can shave, bathe and wash their clothes at the campsite. A dormant mesquite comes in handy as a laundry line.

This particular crew has recently completed their work at the Rose Tree and Babacomari ranches and is now methodically cutting their way through the beargrass plants at the Triangle M Ranch near Elgin. Soon they will move on to the Rain Valley Ranch and from there proceed eastward towards Willcox, Pearce, Safford and Bonita.

An old water barrel sees duty as a makeshift cook-stove. Crockery plates can be seen in the background. This is not communal living. Each man has his own cooking gear and fixes his meal at his tent at the end of the workday.
Barr photo.

Beargrass, nolina microcarpa, also known as basketgrass, is a member of the agave family. Its creamy white flowers bloom in May and June at elevations from 3,000 to 6,500 feet. The grass-like leaves are tough, with no marginal spines and grow up to ½" wide, 4' long in a large basal rosette pattern. Mexicans use the leaves for basketry and Native Americans used the bud stalks for food, according to, "A Field Guide to the Plants of Arizona," by Anne Orth Epple. About 25 or 30 years ago, the Arizona Historical Society brought a team of Papago Indians (now referred to as Tohono O'odham) to cut the grass in this area and give a demonstration of basket weaving at the museum in Tucson.

A full-grown beargrass plant takes up a lot of space, crowding out the native grasses that would feed livestock and wildlife. The animals won't touch the tough spears of the nolina, but once the plant has been cut, the asparagus-like new growth is a delicacy for cattle. Mule deer are also very fond of it and when they smell it, they come for miles to feast on the new shoots. After about 18 months the grass rejuvenates and in three years it is ready to be harvested again. By then, the crew has completed their circuit of ranches and is ready to return to the Sonoita area.

To efficiently cut the tough blades of grass, the workers use a gas-powered machine similar to a weed eater. It has a diamond edged blade that never needs sharpening. When the machines break down, they are repaired on the spot by the head cutter, Hector Manuel Torres, an expert machinist who can get the equipment running again in a short time.

Enrique Huma works with the three donkeys. On one of their sweeps through Sonoita a lion mauled one of his favorite donkeys, Cucho, during the night. The badly injured burro's left nostril was ripped out in the attack. The veterinarian in Agua Prieta put Cucho on penicillin for several months. The indomitable animal made a complete recovery and is now back on the workforce, good as new.

The men rarely take a break from their backbreaking tasks. First they cut around the base of each plant with the gas cutter, and then take a short handled scythe to make the final cut and gather up bunches of grass. When the cutter has a good sized bunch, he shakes it vigorously to remove the chaff, then stands it on end and bangs it once or twice on the ground to settle it down. When he has enough to make a bundle he ties two "ropes" fashioned of knotted grass around the bundle and snugs it up, jumping up on the bundle to get better leverage and yank it even tighter.

This is when Enrique begins the burro-loading process. Each animal is fitted out with a wooden packsaddle, and he puts one of the heavy bundles on each side and then piles one or two more on top. Enrique swings the bundles off and on the burros with the ease that comes from years of practice, but when ranch foreman, Joe Quiroga, tried to lift one of them he said, "I think I'm a pretty strong guy, but I can't even budge this."

Thus loaded down, the burros are led to the pickup spot where the bundles are stacked to await the arrival of the truck. Once the donkeys have seen where the day's bundles will be piled, they unerringly return to that spot for the rest of the day. Enrique is paid $12 per day for his job of loading and leading the burros.

The cutters are paid by weight, just like cotton pickers and other farm workers. The bundles weigh approximately 70 kilos and the cutter receives $43 for every ton he produces. Each cutter has a distinctive way of tying his bundles, which signals how they are stacked at the pickup spot. The scales are located on the truck and the bundles are weighed before being loaded, so that each worker's pay can be calculated. The twice-weekly truckload holds about six tons.

Benjamin Bermudez, a Mexican-American businessman, exports the beargrass to a factory in Agua Prieta, Mexico, where it is cut in 18, 20 and 24" lengths and imported back into the U.S. Agents market it to factories where it is used in the manufacture of household brooms. In recent years, over 85 percent of the brooms manufactured in this country have converted to plastic and even newer technology is being developed in China, according to Bermudez, cutting the demand for his product severely. The once thriving industry that used to employ over 1,500 workers across the border is now (in 2004) down to three factories with 140 employees.

The trend towards synthetic materials, combined with a stagnant labor pool, is of great concern to Bermudez, who has been sending his crews to the Sonoita area for over 25 years. Most of the workers have been with him all that time and are now in their forties and fifties. Since the young men are not interested in this demanding physical labor, Bermudez predicts that soon the beargrass cutters will be nothing more than a faded memory.

Della Honnas on the front porch of her tarpaper shack near the crossroads at Sonoita. Part of the homestead has been developed into an upscale subdivision. Circa late 1930s. Photo courtesy Donald Honnas

Della Honnas

Sonoita

The date was sometime in the late 1800s when Della Peysert arrived in Arizona Territory via horse and buggy. She, her husband, and his sister, Lillian Varner, had traveled from the Cheyenne Bottoms near Big Bend, Kansas, and settled in the Swisshelm Mountains. Peysert laid claim to the Swisshelm Mining and Reduction Company and their son, Cecil, was born in a tent in the mining camp in 1907.

Soon thereafter, Della divorced Peysert and married P. A. Honnas, who adopted young Cecil and raised him as his own. Their grandson, Donald Honnas, has a yellowing copy of a stock certificate showing that M. S. Peysert sold 25,000 shares of stock in the mining company to P.A. Honnas, the only clue to the mysterious triangle of their lives.

The little family subsequently moved to the St. David area where they farmed for several years and then pulled up stakes in 1916 and drove their small herd of cattle to Sonoita, passing through Rain Valley where they had to pay a rancher to water their animals. It was a drought year and water was so scarce that the rancher couldn't afford to let them use up all his water for free. Nine-year-old Cecil attended the old one-room Sonoita School where Mrs. LeGendre, whose husband ran the mercantile store, was his teacher.

Della and her husband scratched out a living on the homestead, located on the northwest corner of the present day crossroads at Sonoita. They raised dairy cows and chickens, planted vegetables and lived in a tarpaper shack. The crumbling remains of the old milk house are still standing just north of the Sonoita Bible Church. Although the area is fenced to keep animals out, vandals have left their mark by spraying graffiti on some of the walls, but the outlines of Della's gardens and the old well are still a visible reminder of bygone days.

According to Cecil's son, Donald Honnas, his grandmother always planted her garden by the signs of the moon. She branded, de-horned and castrated in the same manner, with the help of her son Cecil and his two boys. Butchering was done in cold weather and the meat was hung outside at night. It was then wrapped in sheets or blankets and stored under the bed during the heat of the day.

Della didn't have very many cows and she worked hard to care for them, feeling it was better to do something rather than sit and watch them suffer. "When one sick cow would not eat or drink and wasn't chewing, her diagnosis was that the cow had lost her cud. She would look around the corral for the lost cud but I don't remember her ever claiming to have found it," Donald laughs. "She would force a dirty dishrag down the cow's throat to take the place of the cud and the bacteria on the rag helped her to digest. Sometimes the cow would die and sometimes she would live in spite of the treatment."

A major source of income was their dairy herd and they shipped their cream to Nogales. Some years ago, Donald Honnas was sitting in Zula's Restaurant in Nogales eating a piece of their famous apple pie when Frank Carroon joined him. Donald relates, "Carroon said that my granddad took a shipment of cream in a Model T Ford down to Nogales. He was telling a guy at the creamery that he was short on water. Carroon went in later and the man said to him, 'Do you think that guy is honest. He said he's out of water. He must be waterin' the milk!' I guess he didn't know that cows need water to produce good milk!"

By 1930, Cecil was working as a mechanic at the crossroads in Sonoita. The pretty young schoolteacher from the Empire School came in one day with car trouble. She was earning the grand sum of $150 a month and didn't have enough to pay for repairs. When she returned on payday to settle up her bill, Cecil said she didn't owe anything. They were married on December 21, 1930, in Tucson. Cecil and Lottie Leona Moore Honnas had two sons, Raymond and Donald.

Life on the homestead wasn't much easier for Lottie than it had been in Della's day. She cooked on a wood range and heated irons on the stove, raised a garden, canned fruits and vegetables, churned butter and made cheese. In the early days of her marriage they had an outdoor privy, no electricity and a crank phone.

Donald Honnas at the window of the crumbling ruins of his grandmother's milk house on the original Honnas homestead.
Barr photo.

An oral history by Lottie, published in "Arizona National Pioneer Ranch Histories," tells of the time she and Cecil were building a new home on their property and she was preparing to serve peach cobbler for dessert to the family and workers.

"To my surprise, there was a spoon in the cobbler and it was about half gone. I offered them canned peaches, which I would have to get out of the cellar. Fortunately they had lost interest, which might have saved my life. We discovered Cecil's boots just outside of the kitchen door, and our pistol and some ammunition was gone, as well as Donald's levis.

"Silver change was still on the sink. Wetbacks didn't realize coins were worth anything. Down in the cellar I found bullets for our pistol, some jams that had been opened and eaten, and a large tea towel with groceries tied up in it.

"Meanwhile the Border Patrol had picked up a wetback, who had a loaded pistol and most of our other items in his backpack. He was in jail and that night he asked Sheriff J. Lowe to get the peach cobbler recipe. Moral of the story: to catch a thief, make good peach cobbler."

On another occasion, one of Lottie's hens fell into a 20-foot silo and she announced to grandmother Della that she would go down on a rope to bring it up. She and Cecil had gone into an onyx cave about 15 miles from Sonoita using a rope and she was sure she could duplicate the maneuver, but she forgot one important point: Cecil had tied knots along the rope to keep them from slipping as they descended.

As soon as she slipped over the edge of the silo she lost a glove and because of the missing knots hit bottom fast, badly burning her hand but landing on an old tire, which broke her fall. Della threw down some ointment for her burns and with the help of Cecil's sister set about fashioning a ladder. "When it was finished they lowered it into the silo and I ascended with delight, carrying the old hen and one egg. Mission accomplished!"

By the time Cecil and Lottie were married, his parents had acquired an additional homestead and now had approximately 640 acres of land. Cecil paid about $10 an acre for the land on his first homestead. He and Lottie would pay off a parcel and just as soon as they owned it free and clear they would buy another one. According to Donald, "They were at an opportune time for this because the homesteaders were going broke. They accumulated about 3,500 acres of deeded land." In 1960 they sold 2,300 acres of deeded land to a developer, keeping enough land to run about 40 head of cattle. They donated the land for the Sonoita Bible Church and Cecil personally did the construction work.

Reflecting on her life as a southern Arizona ranch wife, Lottie said, "The things that I appreciate and which have come about in my lifetime on the ranch are eradication of the screwworm, the calf puller, electricity, telephone, and being able to buy eggs, milk and butter at the store." In 1982, Cecil suffered a fatal heart attack while riding the range on his beloved ranch and Lottie moved to a retirement home in Tucson until her death.

Betty Barr

Nikolas and Josefa Yourgules with their older children circa 1935. Front row, left to right: Lena, George, Joe and Isabel. Rear: Frances and Juan.
Photo courtesy Mike Yourgules.

Betty Barr

Mike Yourgules and Norman Hale

Harshaw

The road winds south from Patagonia through rolling curving hills before it veers west to the old mining town of Harshaw. The drought that has plagued southeast Arizona for the past several years has rendered the landscape a dry and dusty brown. However, viewing the scenery through the eyes of a native-born son such as Mike Yourgules turns the brown grass and trees into the lush and verdant hillsides of his youth. He paints a vivid picture of the abundant grasslands, trees and running streams that were the norm in the early 1930s in this beautiful valley.

Mike was born in the San Rafael Valley, the youngest of a large family and the only one delivered by a medical doctor rather than a midwife. The family lived near the Vaca Ranch and raised all their own vegetables in a garden that thrived under the wet conditions prevalent in that era. There was no electricity or running water. All the homes had their own hand-dug well. Water was drawn up and carried to the house in buckets.

His mother, Josefa, well-known in the area for her outstanding cooking, prepared meals on a wood-burning stove. Her tamales were coveted by the surrounding ranchers, especially at Christmastime. The family did not have cattle of their own but mavericks abounded and even pigs were known to roam around untended. The children always wondered if the ranchers who clamored for their mother's famous tamales ever knew where the delicious fillings came from.

To keep food fresh under these conditions, cows were milked morning and night and the milk and cream were used right away. Meat was wrapped in burlap, rolled in canvass and then stored under the bed where it was cool and dark and kept fresh for quite some time. Large beef or game would be made into jerky, stored in clean flour sacks and roasted on the grill months later for a tasty meal. Most houses had a little trap door in the floor that opened to an underground storage area. Fruits and vegetables were wrapped in newspapers or stacked in boxes and, if picked slightly green, would be edible all winter.

A crumbing adobe ruin on the south side of the road marks the location of the old mining town of Harshaw and from there it is just a short drive to our destination, a cluster of adobes and tin-roofed outbuildings known as the Hale Ranch. Norman Hale and his family raise cattle here, just two short miles from the homestead that was first farmed by his grandfather, Richard Farrell in 1915, at what was then known as Dickey's Place.

The Finley house on Harshaw Creek was built by the man who staked the Hermosa Mine. The Hermosa boomed three times and brought many settlers to the area.
Barr photo.

Across Harshaw Creek is the Finley house, an old stone structure built by the man who opened the Hermosa Mine and Mill just over the hill. This mine was the center of the silver boom that started in 1850 and eventually brought over 2,000 people to the area. The town was named for David Harshaw, who founded the Hardshell Mine nearby in 1875.

Not so long ago these hills were dotted with houses and hundreds of families called this valley their home. The mine boomed three times in all, but once it played out, there was no work left and it became a ghost town. Many of the homes were washed away in a big flood and the land has gone back to nature.

Norman was born on the property in 1914 and attended the one-room Harshaw School where one of his teachers was "Old Lady McFarland," Jack Turner's grandmother. She drove a wagon and team from their place near the Rocking Chair Ranch to get to school each day. When Norman was a teenager, his parents sent him to Douglas to live with his aunt and attend high school with his cousin.

The little school in Harshaw burst out of its britches about 1937 when ASARCO took over the mines and brought many more families into the area. By the time Yourgules attended, they had hired a second teacher and added another room onto the school to accommodate the 60 pupils.

Families in isolated homes such as these two grew up in, had to rely on themselves when it came to doctoring for accidents or ailments. Epsom salts, castor oil and Sloane's liniment were standard medicine cabinet items for every ranch house. For boils, Norman's mom would take prickly pear cactus, strip off the thorns, boil the insides and place the warm mixture on the affected area to draw out the core. Ringworm, a common childhood ailment, was treated with "sweat of the axe," placing the metal against the rash to affect a cure. The nearest doctor (in Patagonia) was actually a vet. Norman used to sprain his ankle regularly. He'd soak it, tie it up and go to school on a crutch till it healed. Later he'd fall off the bridge over the creek and go through the same process. He said that was better than calling the vet!

Without TV's to amuse themselves, children came up with their own pastimes. They made slingshots using a forked manzanita branch and practiced shooting small game and birds such as cottontails, raccoons, squirrels and band-tail pigeons. They ate all these critters, but Norman says jackrabbits were a little too tough for his palate. Whole days could be whiled away fishing for minnows or skinny-dipping in the natural pools. Horses were scarce and if a man had a good horse he wouldn't let a kid around it, but everyone had a burro or two and all the kids rode them.

The raucous squawking of Hale's peacocks and guinea hens announced the arrival of Miguel "Mike" Soto, another native of the Harshaw area. He joined the backyard gathering and the three long-time friends shared their recollections of the old days. The most anticipated event of the year in Harshaw was the Festival de San Juan, a day filled with horse and burro races. The only refreshments served were soft drinks, but the men would sneak in some teswin, a homemade cactus brew.

Soto recalled one such night when Manuel Matas, a cowboy from the Mowry Mine, galloped by on his horse and kidnapped Panchita, Yourgules' sister. Norman roared with laughter at the memory. He was only a kid at the time and couldn't imagine why anyone would want to kidnap a girl. In fact, he was wondering when Manuel was planning to return her.

The old adobe house on the way into Hale's place was once owned by Ignacio "Nacho" Arias. He ran a pool hall there and visitors would tie their horses up at the cottonwood tree outside. He made raspodas, a kind of shaved ice, poured canned milk and sugar on top and served it in a cup for five cents. The kids usually didn't have many coins, only what they could filch from the family cookie jar, but if all else failed some of them were known to take the "five-finger discount."

When a big fire threatened the area, the local men were paid $1 a day as firefighters. The Acevedo boys were part of the fire crew and rode over on their prized bay horse. They tied him to a large tree and when they returned, the tree was on fire. The rope was completely fried and the horse was burned on his legs. From that day on, he was referred to as Quemada (the burned one).

Margaret and Jack Jackson, a black couple that lived for a time in the Finley house, came from Fort Huachuca. The kids loved to sit on their porch and listen to Margaret's stories. It was summertime, and her Holstein cow wouldn't come in to milk. The cow had a bell on her and Margaret could hear it wandering around in the cemetery across the way. She wanted her husband to bring the cow home, but he wouldn't do it. Finally she told him, "Jack, you don't have to be afraid of those dead people, it's the live ones you've got to watch out for." Today the cemetery has fallen into disrepair. There is no road leading up to it, so visitors must walk up the hill. Some of the gates have been stolen and many graves are unmarked.

Another ranch owned by Hale is on the road leading into the San Rafael Valley. The former Ernest Best Ranch, it has been the site of several movies. William Holden filmed the Wild Rovers there and shot the opening wedding scene of this made-for-TV movie in the living room of the ranch house.

Life is a lot quieter in Harshaw as the twenty-first century dawns, but Norman and Ruth, his wife of 60 years, still raise cattle there with the help of their daughter, Mary. Their other daughter, Nancy, a retired elementary school teacher, also makes her home on the property. Times may have changed, but the peace and tranquility in this beautiful valley are a timeless reminder of the area's ranching heritage.

Wayne Wright halter breaking a colt at a boy's summer camp at Steamboat Springs, Colorado in 1949. Son John (with back to camera) looks on.
Photo courtesy of Clem Wright

Wayne Wright

Sonoita

"We guided this judge and his daughter on a mule deer hunt in Wyoming, and when we got ready to pack out the meat it was so heavy we were having trouble heaving it up on the pack horse. After several unsuccessful tries, the pack horse got disgusted with us and sat down on his haunches to make it easier." Wayne Wright, one of Sonoita's old-time cowboys chuckles as he recounts how the judge had brought along a professional photographer so that they would have a good memento of his daughter's hunt. The best picture to come out of it wasn't the trophy muley, but the sheepish guides loading a seated packhorse.

Wayne had a little Border collie pup that would get sore-footed and he got in the habit of carrying him up on the saddle on the way home. One day he was out on the trail on a thoroughbred he had just gotten from Dick Jimenez, when it started thundering and little Pete jumped right up in the saddle with him. The startled horse started bucking. Wayne left the saddle and when he looked up the dog was still on the horse. Wayne's wife, Clem, claims that Wayne taught Pete to hold the reins while he got off to doctor a cow or open a gate.

Wayne and Clem were married in Wyoming and the young couple scratched out a living raising sugar beets and alfalfa and catching wild horses that they broke for work or sold to the auction. Their other crop was pinto beans and Clem says, "We wondered what people did with them. We never heard of anyone eating them until we came down here and discovered how good they were."

They moved to Arizona in 1948 when Wayne heard about a job opening in Tucson at the Southern Arizona School for Boys in Sabino Canyon. Clem says the Wyoming winters were so cold and miserable that it only took them about 30 seconds to make up their minds, pack their belongings, drop the unwanted items off at the auction and hit the road for Arizona. Wayne taught the boys to rope, ride western and play polo. He would purchase a string of horses each year and sell them to the boys, who were all required to own and care for a horse during the school year. In spring when school let out, a lot of the horses were sent up to a boys' camp in Steamboat Springs, CO, where Wayne taught ranch classes and Clem was head of housekeeping.

Clem and the owner's wife would often go out for a ride in the late afternoons after their chores were done. Wayne told her if you ever get lost, just give the horse a loose rein and he'll eventually bring you home. When the trail became obliterated in the high ferns she followed his advice and gave the horse his head. Finally they crested a ridge and her friend said, "I see a line of clothes hanging out to dry down there." Clem looked down and recognized her own laundry flapping in the breeze. They could see the house, but it took a while to find a gate in the fence. Clem remembers, "We knew we were close, but we couldn't get there from here."

In the fall it was back to Tucson. After the day's classes were done Wayne would lead the kids on trail rides in the Catalina foothills and once a year on a full-fledged pack trip. They did this twice and the third year the packhorse he was leading kept balking. Wayne took a loop on the end of his rope and wrapped it around the saddle horn to keep him moving forward. They were going around a curve in the trail when the pack got caught on a rock, pulling the horse up short. Wayne's horse was caught off balance and tumbled over the edge. "He rolled over the full length of me. I don't know how I kept from getting killed." It didn't bother the packhorse any; the loop had popped off the saddle horn and he was still up on the trail, completely unfazed by the whole affair. Wayne, however, suffered a shattered shoulder and wasn't able to work for the rest of the year.

After he healed up, he found a position at Apache Springs Ranch near Sonoita, where they stayed for seven years. One time, he and Ralph Spellers went over to the Santa Rita Ranch to butcher hogs and they could hear the Lee Brothers' lion dogs up in Box Canyon. They decided to go over and see if they could help out.

Dale and Clell Lee were well-known hunters that were often called on by ranchers to take care of lions or bears that were killing calves. Dale told them they wanted to capture him for the zoo or movies, so they planned to push the lion down the canyon and when he went up the tree, Dale would put a loop on a rope and flip it over his head.

It took ten tries, but he finally got him. He took a stick, wrapped a string around each side of it, grabbed the lion's mouth and wrapped the string around his chin so he couldn't bite him. Then he tied his feet together, put him in a packsaddle pannier and loaded it on a mule. The mule didn't object to packing out a live mountain lion, he was used to it. The hardest part of the whole operation was getting the angry lion, into a compartment in the pickup truck.

Wayne has ridden a lot of savvy horses in his time. He particularly remembers riding over on the Santa Rita side of the mountain on a horse that was new to him and new to the trail. It was getting dark and they were heading back. Finally, he found the gate and pushed on through. In that utter darkness that occurs just before the moon comes out, the horse refused to go forward. He kept stopping and Wayne couldn't get him to move even when he kicked him in the belly. Finally the moon came out and illuminated their position. They were at the edge of a cliff. Somehow the horse sensed the danger. He kept that horse for a long time.

After two stints working for Keith Brown at Apache Springs Ranch and a brief time with Bud Ewing at the Z Triangle in Canelo, Wayne and Clem settled in Sonoita where he pumped gas for Sam Fraizer for a while. He spent many years at the Fairgrounds in charge of maintenance, provided cattle for the ropings, rode and broke horses for local ranches and drove the school bus for 20 years. Clem helped Ilene Fraizer at the Lunch Room diner, which was, according to Bob Bowman, "The best place in town for bachelors to eat. When the wives were gone, you could go there and get a hamburger, a piece of pie, and a cup of coffee for 50 cents!"

Wayne's favorite all-time horse was old Rocky Bobby. When Jack Buckingham sold the Umpire Ranch the new owners didn't want an old stallion on their pasture, so Jack says, "Why don't you take Rocky Bobby?" He had won the Rocky Mountain Futurity in Denver in 1951, but was so gentle that you could put him out in the pasture and he wouldn't even bother the geldings. People would bring their mares in to be "pasture bred" and he was raring to go, even at age 30. He bred a mare that last morning and was feeling fine. The vet came by and gave him a vitamin shot and he jumped up and ran back to the pasture and all at once he went over backwards and was dead before he hit the ground. "Guess it was just his time to go," Wayne says.

Wayne Wright shows a group of campers at the Whiteman Boys Camp in Steamboat Springs, Colorodo, the proper way to shoe a horse. Wright was in charge of horsemanship at the camp. Son John (at left) watches intently.
Photo courtesy of Clem Wright

Betty Barr

Ilene Fraizer standing in the doorway of the Lunch Room. Sam Fraizer's garage is seen to the left.
Photo courtesy of the Fraizer family.

Ilene Fraizer

Sonoita

Lots and lots of homemade pie dished up with a dash of humor turned out to be a surefire recipe for success for Ilene Fraizer. Dozens of her legendary pies were devoured daily by the ranchers, tourists, and cowboys who frequented her Lunch Room, still others ended up on the dinner tables of friends and neighbors, all served with her trademark quick smile and ever-ready comeback.

Ilene was pretty unflappable and it wasn't easy to get her to lose her cool, but that didn't stop her customers from trying. Like the morning when Reagen Gardner and Frank Hedgcock plopped down at the counter and started badmouthing the cherry pie served at Gardner's home the previous night. Ilene was thinking to herself how rude they were to criticize the wife's cooking, when it suddenly occurred to her that it was one of her pies. With a flare of temper she snapped, "Your wife can make her own d— — pies from now on," as the room erupted in shouts of laughter.

Customers weren't the only ones to try and get the best of Ilene. There were a lot of salesmen who came in regularly and became friends over the years. The Crispy Potato Chips salesman was especially congenial and he and Ilene had a constant bantering going on. One holiday season he appeared bearing a very nice-looking box of candy. He knew she had a special fondness for chocolates and wouldn't be able to resist trying one right away. She immediately opened the box and chose a candy but couldn't bite through it. Not wanting to embarrass him, she very quietly slipped it in the trash and tried another. The second piece proved equally as hard and on closer inspection she discovered they were made of rubber. "I tried for years to repay him, but was never able to top this prank," Ilene laughs.

The Lunch Room evolved in a roundabout way. Back in the late forties, Ilene and her husband Sam built a small house and shop on a corner parcel at the crossroads where the Sonoita Mini Mart now stands. Sam opened a garage, service station and hardware store in December 1946. At that time the Highway Department was realigning Hwy. 82, from Sonoita to Mustang Corners (the highway had previously gone through Elgin). The Fraizer's new house included a large dining room and the construction boss asked Ilene if she would be willing to feed his crew for five or six months while they completed the project.

The 24-year-old Ilene, who had never cooked for anyone but her husband before, soon found herself rising before dawn to feed breakfast to 30 hungry men at 5 a.m. The crew went through gallons of hot coffee, stacks of pancakes and biscuits and dozens of eggs and potatoes. She packed lunches for them the night before and fed them dinner at 6 p.m. She was paid $4.50 to provide the three meals per day for each man and at the end of the month they would present her with a bottle of sloe gin, her favorite drink at the time. The men were kind and considerate and she remembers wryly, "They added greatly to my vocabulary and imagination with their tall tales."

The crew was always bragging about who could consume the hottest chilis, so Ilene decided to give them the acid test. She went across the border in Nogales and purchased the hottest chilis she could find. That night the chilis were passed around and each man would ask, "Are they hot?" No one would admit it until a bald man tried one. The large beads of perspiration running down his bald head proved the point and the requests for hot chilis dropped off remarkably after that.

When the road project was finished five months later, Ilene installed a counter with eight stools and the Lunch Room was born. The menu consisted of hamburgers, sandwiches, individual cans of soup and homemade pies. Coffee was 10 cents a cup, burgers and a slice of pie brought the astounding sum of 35 cents each. The garage was located right next door, which often led to a little confusion. One day a gentleman stuck his head in the door and asked, "Can I get an inner tube?" Ilene quipped, "How do you want it, fried or scrambled?"

In the fifties there were still large caravans of gypsies coming through the area. The gypsies would pile out of their car and swarm all over the place. With Ilene in the Lunch Room, one person busy in the garage and the other person pumping gas, it was impossible to keep an eye on all of them. After they left, tools and other things would turn up missing. "Once was enough," says Ilene. "The next time they appeared, Sam came out armed with his shotgun. After that they didn't stop by very often."

Sam and Ilene met in San Diego where they both worked in an aircraft factory. Ilene was born in Nebraska and came west at the invitation of a girlfriend who was engaged to a friend of Sam's. She told me, "I've got a guy for you," Ilene remembers and adds that Sam told his friends not to introduce them until the day after Christmas because he couldn't afford to buy her a gift. After a whirlwind two weeks, the couple was married in January 1942. They adopted a son and a daughter and the marriage lasted almost 50 years, until Sam's death in 1991.

Sam was born at Fort Huachuca where his father worked as a carpenter. Sam's mother, Carrie Fraizer, and her sister came west in 1914 and homesteaded on the Vaughn Loop Road. The two women, who were unmarried at the time, had only themselves to rely on and Carrie passed this trait of self-reliance on to her son, Sam, who in later years would be known as the "go to" guy in Sonoita. After serving in the Second World War, Sam brought Ilene to Sonoita and they lived at the homestead with his parents until Sam finished building the house and service station.

Sam was the heart of Sonoita according to Bob Bowman, an old friend of the family. "He had a phone, Sonoita 5, when most of the outlying places didn't have one. If anybody had a prob-

Ilene Fraizer and her brother Virgil Maake grew up on a farm in Nebraska in the 1930s. Photo courtesy of the Fraizer family.

lem, no matter what it was, they came to Sam." He did all the wiring at the fairgrounds and also served a term as president. He arranged for a fire truck from Fort Huachuca surplus and was instrumental in starting the volunteer fire department. As Ilene says, "He was a Jack-of-all-trades. He could repair wells, make branding irons and fix electrical problems. When submersible pumps came out Sam sold so many that we won a trip to Amsterdam."

In 1966, after 20 years at the same location, Fraizer lost his lease on the corner property. He purchased 25 acres across from the fairgrounds and built a large building, now known as the County building, for the Lunch Room, hardware store, garage and Texaco station. There they continued their business until retiring in 1979 after 33 years.

According to an article in the *Arizona Daily Star,* Jan. 1, 1979, "The saddest people in Sonoita these days are not the Fraizers. They are the cowpokes, the ranchers and the out-of-towners who will miss Ilene's cooking and Sam's hospitality."

Betty Barr

Housekeeping staff at Los Encinos Guest Ranch. (Second from left) head housekeeper who helped Mrs. Hedgcock hire girls across the line. Center is Labrada, the cook. Circa 1941.
Photo courtesy Frank Hedgcock and Bowman Archives Room.

Betty Barr

Carr and Hedgcock families

Los Encinos Ranch
Sonoita

A small cluster of buildings surrounding a pool on Los Encinos Road are the only remaining trace of what was once a thriving guest ranch operation south of Sonoita. In the 1930s and 40s when wartime travel restrictions were in force, the lure of the romantic west as portrayed on the silver screen brought visitors flocking to the dude ranches of southeastern Arizona in record numbers.

Many, such as the Circle Z and Rail X Ranches, were quite elegant, but according to Frank Hedgcock, whose parents owned the Los Encinos Guest Ranch in the early '40s, "We were more rustic. When we first started we had stoves. The cowboys would go in the rooms in the morning and start fires for the guests until we finally put in butane for heating."

The original site of Los Encinos Ranch is now a subdivision a few miles from the Sonoita Crossroads, but back in 1933 when Neil and May Carr purchased the property for $13,600, there were rolling grasslands as far as the eye could see. Carr, a native of England and a graduate in forestry from Oxford, had migrated to the American west after contracting tuberculosis in a POW Camp in Germany. He ended up in Douglas, Arizona, where he met May, a fellow English immigrant. As their son John relates it, it was inevitable. "Two people in Douglas, Arizona, both from

England. They were probably the only people in Cochise County who could understand each other."

The couple settled in Sonoita where as John Carr remembers, his parents had to handle every emergency themselves because of the remoteness of the area. In addition to all the routine ranch chores, Neil Carr usually vetted his own animals and even set a two-year old horse's leg. He kept a large bull snake in the attic to keep the rat population down. There was an old barn on the property made from railroad ties. It caught fire and once it got going there was no way to put it out and it burned to the ground. Carr put in the swimming pool himself and also constructed an oiled tennis court with stripes painted on it.

Soon after purchasing the ranch the Carrs adopted two babies, John and Wendy, who were born just eleven days apart on the seventh and

Neil Carr combs the cockleburs from a horse's tail. Circa 1939.
Photo courtesy John Carr

eighteenth of September. As John laughingly tells it, "We always celebrated our birthday on Sept. 12, and I was ten years old before I found out my real birthday." The children were home-taught by Mrs. Sylvia Watson until third grade when they enrolled at the Sonoita one-room school. They would ride their horses to school and turn them loose in the pasture during class. According to Wendy Carr (Potter), "I rode Bessie because she was small and I could get on her, but I couldn't catch her. The fourth graders got out early and the Dojaquez boys would catch my horse for me."

Their happy days on the ranch came to a jarring halt in 1943 when Neil Carr got into a disagreement with some of his employees over a load of firewood. In the ensuing argument, he was bludgeoned to death. Two men were charged with the crime but there were court delays due to the war and the case never went to trial.

Harvey and Lydia Hedgcock, frequent guests at the ranch, purchased Los Encinos from Carr's widow the following year. The following year they invited Harvey's brother Houghton "Bum" and his wife, Francis, to become partners in the operation.The Hedgcock Building at the Fairgrounds is named in Bum's honor.

They eventually bought up some small adjacent homesteads, acquired forest permits and began a cattle operation in conjunction with the dude ranch. In all they ran about 167 head on 2,000 acres of land. The guest ranch was a year round operation and, "in November we would include the guests in the round-up. They also went out and participated in the spring branding and so forth," Frank (the son of Bum and Frances) said, noting that this practice has become even more popular today.

Harvey Hedgcock, co-owner with his brother Bum of Los Encinos Guest Ranch, in the tack room. Coati mundi skin on the wall. 1944.
Photo courtesy Patti Hedgcock Smith and Bowman Archives Room.

The main lure of a dude ranch of course is the horses and the Hedgcocks had a good string of reliable mounts and two wranglers to help with the trail rides. According to Frank, "Some of the horses would bow up a little and so we'd ride them down, but most of them were just gentle old horses."

A strict rule was that you did not take the guests out alone or you'd be in a heap of trouble. Nevertheless, Harvey's daughter, Patti Hedgcock Smith says, "I took it upon myself to take two of the young guests riding. I wanted to show them Roosevelt Cave." The wranglers had taken Patti to this cave out near Papago Springs several times before. There was a great big room with a hole like a tunnel and the cowboys would grab some bear grass, fold it up and light it so they could see their way inside.

Patti was curious to explore it further, so she brought along a flashlight and the three youngsters crawled in until they reached a spot where the trail branched in two directions, and they were afraid to go further. Suddenly the young boy guest was overcome with an asthma attack and things got a little dicey. Patti realized no one knew where they were, their horses might have gotten untied and they could be in serious jeopardy. Luckily, they finally crawled back out and returned home safely with no one the wiser.

Another favorite activity was the western style cookouts held in a grove not far from the house. The standard chuckwagon fare of steak, beans and tortillas was supplemented with a favorite of the guests' dubbed "Sonoita Smear," named for the compound used to treat cattle for worms. It consisted of caramelized condensed milk, graham crackers and peaches with whipped cream. The guests loved it, but to the wranglers it was always known as "Smear 62."

By 1949, Harvey had fallen ill and Bum bought out his interest in the ranch. The end of the war signaled a resumption of foreign travel and the guest ranch business slowed down. Bum decided to get out of the dude and cattle business and converted the guest quarters into single family houses for rentals. Many locals such as Wag and Marie Schorr and Bob and Sally Grennan rented there while they were building their own homes. In 1959 the entire ranch was sold to Don Millstone, a Tucson developer and real estate broker.

Betty Barr

Anne called her favorite picture "The Three Grays."
Paul Mahalik photo, courtesy Bowman Archives Room.

Anne Stradling

Patagonia

Ask six different people what Anne Stradling was really like and there will be six divergent answers. She was the visionary developer, the generous philanthropist, the rough and ready hard-as-nails cowgirl, the daredevil pilot and trick rider, the rebellious socialite, the quick-tempered employer. But one thing they all agree on, Anne's great and lifelong passion was horses.

Born into a wealthy New Jersey family, Anne never quite fit into the socialite mold, according to Bernie Solsberry, her personal representative. Her father was president of the prestigious Far Hills Hunt Club, but the real equestrienne of the family was her mother. An early photograph shows Mrs. Schley skillfully driving a team of mules in tandem; quite a feat considering that the lead mule has no traces and is only connected to the follow mule and the driver by a thin leather lead. Basically he is free.

Anne's family owned Rogers Locomotive and had ties to Bethlehem Steel. Her parents traveled extensively throughout Africa and the Orient collecting priceless objets d'art, which filled their beautiful mansion. Anne was sent to a succession of expensive private boarding schools, but studying was never a priority with her and her antics, such as riding her horse into the girl's dormitory at night, caused her family much embarrassment. Finally, despairing of ever reforming their high spirited daughter, they set her up with a generous trust fund enabling her to go west where she joined up with the Miller Brothers 101 Wild West Show.

The Millers owned a large Oklahoma ranch, so named because it covered 101 sections (not acres) of prime ranch land. The brothers had bought out the partnership of Buffalo Bill and Pawnee Bill when those two had fallen on hard times. They renamed the show after their ranch and it was there that Anne met her first husband who taught her the ropes of trick riding. That marriage failed and she soon hooked up with another trick rider. When the Wild West show folded, Anne purchased the Miller Brothers 101 Ranch where her daughter ended up living many years later.

Anne was the legendary founder of the Museum of the Horse, the main tourist draw for many years in Patagonia. Much of the interesting western memorabilia in the Museum of the Horse came from the 101 Ranch, which was so large that it had its own saddle shop. One of their handmade saddles was displayed in the Museum along with a stagecoach that Anne found under a tree there and had shipped to Patagonia to be repaired and put on display.

When Anne met Floyd Stradling, her third husband, he was drilling wells in South America. Floyd was from a ranching family in northern Arizona and was a kind, polite, soft-spoken cowboy, in sharp contrast to Anne whose refined background was belied by her rough and tumble ways and colorful language. When his drilling job was complete, the couple moved to Tucson and then decided to look around for some cattle property. This brought them to Patagonia and the KJ Ranch on Harshaw Road owned by Kenneth (Bill) and Jane Holbrook. To their mutual amazement, Jane and Anne discovered that they had known each other at Fermenta, a private boarding school in Aiken, South Carolina. This casual early relationship blossomed into a lifelong friendship after the Stradlings purchased the Holbrook's ranch and moved into the valley, according to Jane's daughter, Patty Oliver. This was the first of several ranch properties that Floyd and Anne operated over the years. They also bought the Bergier Ranch on Harshaw Road, an irrigated pasture and ranch in Elfrida and another property behind the high school in Patagonia.

In early 1960, Anne decided to open a motel and restaurant in Patagonia and eventually built the Museum of the Horse and the adjoining gift shop. It caused some controversy in the town when she tore down the Patagonia Commercial Company to build The Stage Stop Motel, especially since it included a bar much too close to the Seventh Day Adventist Church. But Anne managed to complete the project and for many years her museum served as a magnet for tourism and trade for

Anne Stradling driving her buggy, was a familiar sight in Patagonia in the 1960s. Her Museum of the Horse was donated to the Museum of the American West in Ruidoso, New Mexico in 1992. Photo courtesy Stradling Equine Foundation.

the local economy. The museum was a virtual treasure trove of western art, sculpture and artifacts, many from her family collection and a huge array of Indian jewelry and pottery. Her father was a personal friend of both Remington and Russell and owned several of their original paintings and bronzes, some of which have never been reproduced.

Stradling owned an old adobe building adjacent to the Stage Stop Inn, and rather than demolish it, she completely enclosed it with a Butler building. The adobe building, metal roof and all, can still be seen inside. She had 46 horse-drawn vehicles that needed refurbishing, and designed a living history museum where visitors could view the blacksmith repairing the vehicles that would eventually go on display. In

1973, she brought in Doug Thaemert to build the room in the back and construct a blacksmith shop where visitors could see an old craft being done with period tools.

Thaemert also built the Museum's cattle and mining exhibits, and an old style wooden shoeing floor with a leaning wall where he shod horses using shoes and nails made on the premises. The horse would stand horizontally to the wall and then lean against it while the farrier worked on him. He was then turned and tied the opposite way for the other side to be worked on. Although all the exhibits were sent to a museum in Ruidosa, NM, upon Stradling's death, the shoeing floor and remnants of the shop still remain to this day.

Driving carts and buggies was one of Anne's favorite things to do, but sometimes it got her into a jam. On one occasion, George Yakobian, president of the Patagonia Rotary Club at the time, invited Sen. Barry Goldwater to speak to the group at a luncheon at the Stage Stop. Goldwater flew in to Nogales Airport on the first leg of his re-election campaign, and was picked up at the edge of town by Stradling, driving a horse drawn surrey. Also along for the ride were Yakobian and H. B. Thurber, a prominent local cattleman.

A crowd of about 100 people lined the streets as they pulled up in front of the Stage Stop, when suddenly the horse spooked violently, knocking the buggy over on its side and dragging it down the only paved street in town. Thurber, at age 85, still had the presence of mind to jump off to the left as the buggy tipped to the right. Goldwater was dumped out and Anne Stradling landed smack on top of him. An August 31, 1974, *Arizona Republic* article quoted Goldwater as joking, "I'd do this any day if she would fall on top of me." Meanwhile, Yakobian was trapped in the buggy and his arm was being dragged along the pavement. According to George, "The whole thing seemed to happen in slow motion. The only other time I got that 'slo-mo' feeling was in the Philippines."

Among the bystanders was cattleman Bob Bowman, who leaped to the rescue, grabbing the panicked horse and getting him under control. No one was seriously injured, and after being declared fit by Dr. Delmar Mock, Goldwater and party retired to the "Feedlot" dining room in the Stage Stop where Yakobian encouraged his fellow Rotarians to "Vote Republican" in the upcoming election.

Other driving stories abound. Marie Schorr remembers many Christmases when Anne would hitch up her team, load the wagon with gaily-wrapped gifts and drive through town delivering presents to her friends and fellow townspeople. When Peter Robbins from the Little Outfit Ranch was to be married in a Nogales church,

Anne and her buggy were again pressed into service. Bob Bowman relates that she picked up the bridal couple, the groom resplendent in swallowtail coat and top hat, and drove them to the church in fine western style.

Anne Stradling died in 1992, but her legacy lives on in the community. The Anne C. Stradling Foundation that was established by her Will has provided funding for the expensive lighting at the County Fairgrounds, making nighttime events possible, and supports youth and equestrian related activities in the local area.

Lopez Pool Hall, a landmark in Patagonia, now houses Doug Thaemert's blacksmith shop. Barr photo.

Betty Barr

Lopez Pool Hall

Patagonia

On a dusty street in Patagonia a long low adobe building sporting the shingle, "Lopez Pool Hall," sits in the sun, inviting a closer look. In years past this historic structure served the community as a bar, pool hall, and bordello. The doors running down the west side opened into cribs for the patrons of the establishment. Local legend has it that the proprietor "found the Lord" one day and banished gambling and drinking from the premises. The room at the far western end became a barber-shop and the others were remodeled into rental apartments. The girls had to find other accommodations.

Today, the building serves as a blacksmith shop and is chock full of interesting antiques, but some vestiges of the old pool hall days still remain. The original bar is just inside and a low wooden arched door leads into the onetime beer cooler that now serves as owner, Doug Thaemert's, library housing his extensive collection of historical books and documents on western freighting and transportation.

The main room bursts at the seams with all kinds of horse drawn vehicles in various stages of restoration. The walls are covered from floor to ceiling with old tools, metal signs and wagon parts, and hanging from the ceiling is a tremendous collection of hitch artifacts. The largest vehicle being restored is a huge chuck wagon, whose trappings are on loan to the Bisbee Museum.

One unusual carriage seat, called a large body, has hearts cut out of the wood on the sides. Thaemert is raising the legs to the traditional 17" chair height and restoring it for seating in his own home. A child's-size cutaway sleigh, a wonderful circus horse, and buggies in various states of restoration fill the room. The collection includes horseless carriages, including a seat and a mother-in-law seat from a 1908 two-cylinder Staver, wheels from a Model T with wooden spokes, and a 1920s trailer kit.

All of this is the brainchild and "baby" of Doug Thaemert who came to Patagonia in 1973 at the request of Anne Stradling to construct and man a living blacksmith exhibit for her Museum of the Horse. Thaemert constructed a complete blacksmith shop where visitors could see an old craft being done with period tools and also built the Museum's cattle and mining exhibits.

Once the museum became full of exhibits it was impractical to continue the smithing operation on the premises. Thaemert moved the shop to its current location, which he purchased from Stradling who by this time had acquired it from the Lopez estate. Along with several others he then opened Southwest Wagon & Wheel Works.

Thaemert is a true steward of local lore, so it comes as no surprise to find that he took extraordinary measures to preserve the history of the Lopez Pool Hall sign when he started his new business. They wanted to paint over the old sign and hang their own shingle, but first they put a transparent grid on the Lopez sign and photographed through it. Because the paint was fading they applied a wetting agent, scribed each letter exactly and took color samples. After the business dissolved, Thaemert was able to recreate the old sign in exact detail. After several years, it is starting to peel and crack a little and has just the proper degree of aging to suit his sensibilities.

Thaemert was born in Denver and as the oldest grandson in the family, he got to spend his summers on his grandfather's farm in Kansas where he began his love affair with farm and plow instruments. There was a complete blacksmith shop on the farm and he loved to hang out there as a boy and study all the strange tools and funny shaped things in the cool, dark shop. After graduation with a business degree from Western State College in Gunnison he worked in both Denver and Washington, D.C., then returned west to open a western clothing, feed, tack and saddle shop in Taos before succumbing to the smithing bug.

Doug is an historian of note and has an extensive collection of local memorabilia that he hopes one day will be displayed in a museum depicting the mining and cattle industry of the Patagonia area. A jail tree complete with leg irons and chain came from the town of Crittendon. The town, founded by John Smith, was located just 2.7 miles east of Patagonia on the way to Sonoita. Towns without a proper jail put leg irons on prisoners and chained them to a tree to prevent escape. The stump of this old mesquite was given to Thaemert by one of Smith's granddaughters who knew of his desire to collect items of local provenance for a future museum.

The original wooden sign from the old Mowry Mine, erected by a group of historical researchers calling themselves The Dons, gives a brief history of the mine. Lt. Sylvester Mowry was accused of Confederate sympathies and imprisoned at Fort Yuma. The mine was taken over by the U.S. Government and Mowry died in London in 1871. An overhead trolley and ore bucket from the Flux Mine, railroad tracks and spikes collected from the mine beds between Patagonia and Sonoita, a set of safe deposit boxes from the old Patagonia Bank, a bench that is the identical mate to the one on display at the Patagonia Railroad Depot, brass fronted Post Office boxes, a two-man windlass, many small ranch and mining tools and numerous photos round out the collection.

Impressive gates at the entrance to Black Oak Pioneer Cemetery were donated to the community by Ida Speed Turney.
Barr photo.

Betty Barr

Black Oak Pioneer Cemetery

Canelo

Almost hidden in the wooded rolling hillsides of the Canelo Hills, a simple wrought iron sign marks the turnoff to the Black Oak Pioneer Cemetery. Legend has it that Mexicans approaching these beautiful hills from the south called them Canelo, Spanish for cinnamon, because their light brown color reminded them of the spice.

Four massive stone pillars support elaborate iron gates marking the entrance. The gates were a donation from Ida Turney in memory of her husband Mark and her parents, Ernest and Minnie Speed, old time pioneers of this area.

Once inside, a path to the right puts the visitor in a virtual time warp. The burial plots in this section, some dating as far back as 1902, are eloquently evocative of rural life and death in a bygone time, when men would gather at the cemetery a little early to help with the digging and the headstones were handmade and decorated by family and friends.

Some of the graves are mounded and outlined with large rocks from the surrounding washes. Simpler graves are marked only by a large stone with names and dates of birth and death crudely scratched on the surface. Numerous tiny graves offer mute testimony to the hardships endured by the early settlers.

Toward the rear of the ten-acre parcel, the tree-studded hill slopes off with panoramic vistas of the Canelos and Huachucas to the south and east. In this section, the gravestones and plots are positioned to face the mountains, with their backs to the path. The property is still part of the Forest Service, which allows no trees or bushes to be removed unless they are diseased or dying and the ground cannot be cleared for rows of plots as in a traditional cemetery.

One of the most charming aspects of Black Oak is the distinct personality of each grave. While there are strict requirements as to who may be considered a pioneer and so become eligible to be buried here, there seem to be few such restrictions on the design of the tombstones themselves. Many of the families made and/or decorated their own gravestones. Even in the newer sections, the decidedly rural flavor of this wonderful resting place is evident in the many markers etched with horses, calves, boots or saddles. Still others are fashioned of horseshoes or unusual pieces of metal. Some have miniature grottoes with religious statues; still others are inscribed with poems describing the love of nature and wildlife shared by these pioneer families.

Funerals, such as Mal Eason's, have become the stuff of local legends. The owner of the Umpire Ranch in Canelo now the home of Patti and Andy Kelly, Eason was born in 1876 and achieved fame as the first major leaguer to pitch a no run, no hit game. Marie Schorr, who at that time lived on the adjoining Canelo Hills Ranch, often saw Eason walking down the road with a pick and shovel. She finally learned he was walking the five miles to the cemetery to dig his own grave. The grave-digging project took several years to complete and when he was done, he covered the excavation with a large sheet of metal to keep it from caving in. He found a hollowed out rock, reminiscent of a baseball mitt, which he lugged into place and paired with a round stone just the size of a baseball. This became his headstone, which today rests on a huge cement base.

When Eason passed away at age 94, many in the community turned out for the services. Marie Schorr remembers, "When Wag and I got to the gates of Black Oak, Alex Gonzales was standing there and told us that according to Mal's wishes, no ladies were allowed to see him being interned in the ground. He pointed a short distance away where I could stand with a few other ladies."

Mal's nephew, Fred Purcell Eason, went him one better. The marker of this dedicated sportsman and hunter is sunk in the ground with a trophy elk rack embedded at the top and a miniature airplane and directional device set at the bottom. Alan Lee Eason's grave is in the same style, but emphasizes fishing - a rod complete with a bright red lure stands erect, surrounded by deer antlers, and complete with a hook and bobber securely fastened to the juniper tree that overhangs the site.

Pitcher Mal Eason's grave marker is a metate that reportedly reminded him of a baseball mitt and ball. Eason's barn at the Umpire Ranch in Canelo is pictured on the cover of this book.
Barr photo.

In sharp contrast is the simple marble slab that marks the final resting place of Mark "Bill" Turney, whose wife donated the entry gates. Bill worked for the Vails at the Empire Ranch. As a young man he was involved in a gunfight that cost him his leg, but he never considered giving up the cowboy life. He was so agile that he could hop hard on his left leg, grab the saddle horn and swing his stump over the saddle. Out on the range alone one day, he got trapped afoot after roping a bull. The enraged bull was "on the prod" and every time Bill would get close enough to his horse to attempt to mount, the bull would charge and send him hopping all over the field. His good roping horse kept the bull at bay and after several hours he managed to get back aboard safely. Stone Collie solved Turney's problem by making him a black willow crutch to hook over his left arm, leaving his right hand free for roping and saving him from future one-legged misadventures.

A short way farther along, another simple stone announces the final resting place of Kit Hutchinson. Kit and her husband owned the Little Outfit Ranch and started a one-room school there. After the regular term, the school operated as a summer camp for the rest of the year. The summer kids learned horseback riding and camping and an added bonus was musical productions. Kit had traveled to New York one season and seen Oklahoma performed on stage. She returned to the San Rafael Valley and adapted the music to fit the abilities of her pupils. Talented local musicians Fern Collie and Alvessa Hummel were pressed into service, a stage was set up at the back of the schoolhouse and families came from all around the valley to sit on the hillsides for a live rendition of the famous stage show.

A very impressive stone across the path stands watch over two enormous metates set in concrete. The inscription reads Mattie Riggs Johnson, Oct. 6, 1872 – Jan. 26, 1939. Mattie was an old-fashioned cattlewoman who worked all the cattle herself, always riding sidesaddle. According to local lore, Mattie could ride sidesaddle as well or better than any man could ride astride. Her leases encompassed many acres in the area around the Black Oak and she made special arrangements with the Forest Service to donate part of her lease for the creation of this pioneer cemetery.

One of many veterans buried in Black Oak is Stone Collie, whose two daughters, Jane Woods and Marka Moss, are my guides on our stroll through this beautiful and tranquil place. Stone was a corporal in the army in World War I and he and his wife, Fern Bartlett Collie, ran the Mustang Ranch, which had been homesteaded by Fern's parents in the early 1900s. The Collies later operated it as a cattle and dude ranch. The movie "Oklahoma" was filmed at the train station in nearby Elgin and although the stars drove in from the Santa Rita Hotel in Tucson every day, some of the other actors stayed at the Mustang.

Truly one of a kind best describes the grave of Thomas Heredia, a well-known local cowboy. The marker is fashioned of horseshoes in the shape of a cross with a metal scroll mounted on it. Many other early county leaders and memorable charac-

Many tombstones portray the rancher's way of life, such as this one of Henry and Mary Pyeatt. The Pyeatt family has ranched in southern Arizona since 1882.
Barr photo.

ters can be found here, such as Cora Everhart, teacher, superintendent of schools and secretary of the Santa Cruz County Fair and Rodeo Association; Gilbert "Red" Sanders, well-known roper from the Sands Ranch; Dorothy Stoddard Knipe, who Marka Moss remembers as a lovely lady with her long hair braided and wrapped around her head in a coronet; Sam and Fay Hill who ran a Hereford ranch where Sonoita Hills is located today; Edward and Pearl LeGendre, who ran the general store at the Crossroads where the miners from Greaterville would trade their gold dust for groceries; Gene and Alvessa Hummel; Buster Pyeatt, whose homestead at West Gate is the oldest ranch in the county still owned by the original family; Henry Wood, foreman at the Rail X Ranch whose son, Mack, homesteaded on the Vaughn Loop Road; John Gates, manager at the Heady Ashburn and Vaca Ranches, and Ray "Pete" Barnes, who ran the train from Fairbanks to Patagonia.

In 1917, Mattie Riggs Johnson, who owned the cattle lease on the property, petitioned the Forest Service for an allotment of a ten-acre parcel to be used as a rural cemetery. Her son, James Finley, donated a large sum to permanently endow the cemetery and in 1962, erected a lovely open-air roofed chapel where services can be conducted. As the area became more populated, the demand on the cemetery increased to such an extent that in 1971 it was incorporated and is now governed by a board, which oversees maintenance and assignment of the plots.

The group meets once a year, just prior to Memorial Day, for a potluck lunch and afterwards everyone pitches in to clean up the gravesites. Several times a year a crew of young people, armed with a mower, do a general spruce up. The plots are offered free of charge to pioneer families who lived in the area prior to December 31, 1952, or who have relatives already buried at Black Oak.

Betty Barr

Snow covered hills and a holiday wreath offer the promise of Christmas, at the memorial for Brian O'Regan and his son Michael on Fish Canyon Road.
Barr photo

Betty Barr

Roadside memorials

Santa Cruz County

Roadside memorials, descansos or resting places in Spanish, have been an integral part of the Arizona highway scene for many years. Nowhere is that so evident as in southeastern Arizona. On Hwy 83 between I-10 and Sonoita there are no less than eight such markers, four of them within a short three-mile stretch of the Pass. Several more dot the landscape between Sonoita and Nogales and an actual grave with a simple wooden tombstone is located just off Hwy 83 in the dirt lane behind the Sonoita Realty.

"The first descansos were resting places where those who carried the coffin from the church to the camposanto paused to rest. "Led by the priest or preacher and followed by mourning women dressed in black, the procession made its way from the church to the cemetery. If the camposanto was far from the church, the men grew tired and they paused to rest, lowering the coffin and placing it on the ground. The place where they rested was the descanso." From "Descansos: An Interrupted Journey," by Rudolfo Anaya, Juan Estevan Areliano and Denise Chavez .

Although not a true descanso, the grave near Sonoita marks the site of a sudden and tragic loss for the early day community. Its history has been passed down by word of mouth and according to local storyteller Wayne Wright, "I'm probably the only one around here that still knows the details. Frank Kellogg told me the story. His father witnessed the accident and helped bring the body back to the camp and

271

dig the grave." It was over a hundred years ago, about 1904. The infamous Sonoita winds were blowing then just as strongly as they do today. Southern Pacific Railroad had a construction crew camped near the present day crossroads while they repaired bridges that had been washed out in a flood.

The crew was working about five or six miles west of town, when Albert Hull was blown off a trestle by a tremendous gust of wind, breaking his neck. The story became a local legend and the grave was treated with respect and carefully maintained by Ed LeGendre who had purchased the parcel of land when the railroad shut down. In the early '60s, Ed Pruitt bought the property, planted cottonwoods and Italian cypress around the grave to keep people from driving over it, and installed an irrigation system. The simple brown wood marker, shaped like an old-fashioned tombstone has a red reflector light mounted on the side, but the ravages of time have completely obliterated Hull's name and the inscription.

Historically, descansos have marked the graves of Conquistadors, pioneers and others who died while traveling. The custom is said to go back to pre-Spanish days in the Pimeria Alta (what is now Southern Arizona and Northern Sonora). According to historical documents dating back to 1783, "Fray Antonio de los Reyes, the first Bishop of Sonora, was concerned about the custom of erecting crosses where travelers had been killed by Apaches. The internal combustion engine, in combination with alcohol, has replaced the Apaches as the prime source of sudden death, but the crosses are still with us." From "Beliefs and Holy Places," by James S. Griffith. Today descansos do not signify a place of rest, but a moment of loss for people of all ethnic backgrounds. Although many states outlaw the practice feeling it may distract drivers, others believe they remind drivers to be careful and offer survivors a way to express the human need to mourn and remember.

As Thomas Mann so eloquently stated, "A man's dying is more the survivor's affair than his own." Close observation of the area's memorials shows this to be true. Each shrine has its own personality and many, such as the one at the turnoff to Santa Rita Road in Sonoita, with rough timber steps leading up to the hillside memorial, seem to beckon an invitation to the passing stranger.

According to custom, a jar of artificial flowers and a votive candle are usually found keeping vigil in front of a cross. The cross itself may range in style from a simple design handcrafted of wood, to more durable metals with intricate filigree or more rarely, elegant marble.

Extremely elaborate, but very difficult to find, is the two-fold memorial outside

Officer Brian Johnson's elaborate marble marker is decorated with pumpkins in the fall. No matter what the season, his memory is kept alive with an array of flowers, flags, pinwheels and a miniature ASU football helmet.
Barr photo.

of Nogales at MP 13. A cross with a floral wreath near the road overlooks a steep cliff. At the bottom of the cliff is a magnificent marble cross, at least four feet high but completely hidden from view of the passing motorists. Drainage pipes have been laid on the hill to direct rainwater to the site, which is outlined with large rocks. A feed bucket is attached to the overhanging tree. (Note: This extremely dangerous section of the highway has been the scene of several fatal accidents and there is no safe place to pull over. To find the site, one must be willing to park a distance down the road and hike back).

Although roadside memorials are situated in plain view along the highway for friends and strangers alike to reflect upon, some, such as the simple handmade marker on Hwy 83 in the Pass, contain meanings known only to their loved ones. The cryptic message is hand lettered in orange and simply states: "Thelma and Louise live. Hearts are not broken." The meaning is left to the traveler's imagination.

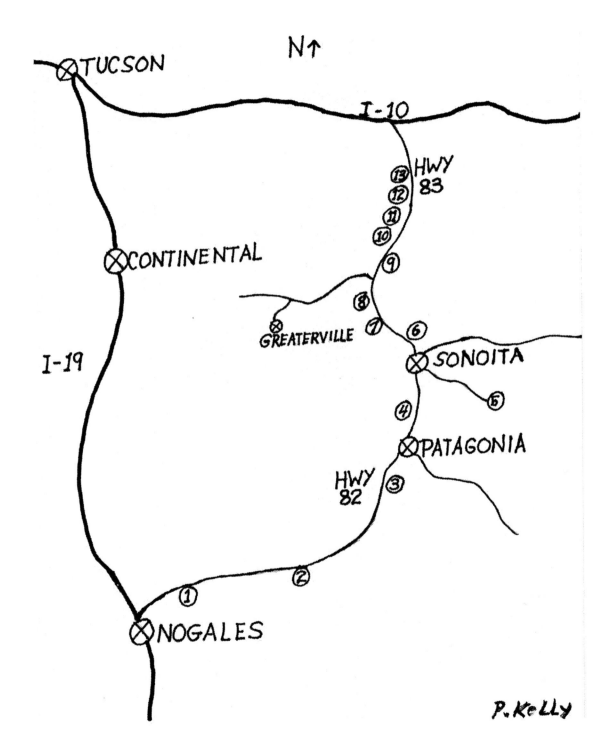

Map: With MP numbers and names by Patti Kelly:

Rte. 82:
1. MP 7S, Chris McGuinness
2. MP 13S, Liliama, 1-26-63 – 12-16-01
3. MP 18S, Sheriff Deputy Pat Thompson
4. MP 22N, Antonio Leon

Rte 83:
5. MP 33E, Albert Hull, Circa 1901
6. MP 34E, Sam Musick,
7. MP 34W, Rudy Rodriguez
8. MP 37W, Brian and Michael O'Regan, 9-02-90
9. MP 44E, Thomas Hicks, 5-04-70 - 2-20-00
10. MP 45W, Thelma & Louise, 1998
11. MP 46W, Officer Brian C. Johnson, 12-13-70 - 3-17-01
12. MP 47W, Steven Matthew Fink, 3-31-80 - 5-06-98
13. MP 54W, Steve Heath 1-25-49 - 11-21-01

Although an effort has been made to include every memorial on the corridor from I-10, via Rte 83 to Sonoita, and from Sonoita along Rte 82 to Nogales, some are hidden or obscured by underbrush and may have been unintentionally over-looked.

Bibliography

Anaya, Rudolfo; Areliano, Juan Estevan; Chavez, Denise, "Descansos: An Interrupted Journey." Del Norte, 1995.

"Arizona National Pioneer Ranch Histories." Arizona Livestock Association, Ca 1960.

Barnes, Will C., "Arizona Place Names." University of Arizona Press, 1988.

Epple, Anne Orth, "Field Guide to Plants of Arizona." Falcon Press, 1995.

Griffith, James S., "Beliefs and Holy Places." University of Arizona Press, 1992.

Piper, Posy, "History of Ranching in Santa Cruz County Arizona. Santa Cruz County Cowbelles Ranchers' Heritage Center, 2004.

Sherman, James E. and Barbara H., "Ghost Towns of Arizona." University of Oklahoma Press, 1969.

Stewart, Janet Ann, "Arizona Ranch Houses, Southern Territorial Styles, 1867 – 1900." University of Arizona Press and Arizona Historical Society, 1974.

Varney, Philip, "Arizona Ghost Towns and Mining Camps." Arizona Highways Books, 1994.

Glossary

Terms and phrases, some with Spanish/Mexican origins, commonly used in the rural and ranching communities of Santa Cruz County.

Bota: Spanish origin, leather wine/water bag.

Brushy country: Thick scrub pine and manzanita terrain, nearly impenetrable and difficult for horses to traverse.

Dally: After roping a calf, the cowboy quickly wraps his rope (dallies) around the saddle horn. If he is not fast enough, he may lose a finger in the process (see "hard and fast").

Desert cooler: A cupboard made of slat shelves with burlap on all sides and on the door. A pan of water with holes sat on top and dripped the water over the burlap. As the breeze blew through, it cooled things down. The legs of the cupboard were set in cans of water to discourage ants and other insects.

Dewlap: Pendulous fold of skin under throat of bovine animal.

Dogie: A motherless calf.

Gathering: Periodic roundup to inoculate, brand and castrate cows and calves.

Gringo: From Spanish, foreigner, not Mexican.

Hard and fast: Cowboy ties end of lariat, "hard and fast," around his saddle horn, before roping calf, to reduce danger of losing a finger (see dally).

Less-chance boys: During the Great Depression many orphaned or very poor children, called less-chance boys, were given jobs with the Civilian Conservation Corps.

Metates: From Spanish, flat stone used for grinding corn.

Nopal/tuna: From Spanish, prickly pear cactus.

Prove up: According to the Homestead Act of 1862, each 60-acre parcel claimed had to be "proved up." The rules stated that the homesteader had five years to live and build a dwelling on the parcel and cultivate at least 40 acres before he would be given free and clear title to the land.

Reata: From Spanish, A lariat made by the Mexican vaquero, by cutting a continuous, circular strip from a large cowhide. The resulting strings would be hung on the fence to dry and then braided with other strips to form a leather lasso.

Remuda: Extra mounts or saddle horses for each cowboy, herded together. An outfit of eight to ten men would require a remuda of up to 100 geldings.

Sore-backed: An adjective describing a painful condition for a horse that has been ridden overly long and hard.

Vaquero: From Spanish, a cowboy, usually of Mexican descent.

Windlass: A device for handling or lifting, especially as used in wells, consisting of a barrel on which the hoisting rope winds with the aid of a hand-operated crank.

Index

Symbols

101 Ranch 254

A

A Triangle Ranch 195
A-7 Ranch 207, 208
Acevedo boys 232
Acevedo, Henry 21
Acevedo, Paul 21
Ajo Mountains 195
Altar, Mexico 47
Alto 25, 28, 30, 33, 34, 35, 36, 37, 40, 42
Alto Camp 26, 40, 50
Alto Cemetery 35
Alto Post Office 39
Alto School 28
Amado 173
AmeriCorps 149
Ammerman, Minnie 25
Anamax 170
Anderson, Mr. 190
Andre, Bruce 185
Anne C. Stradling Foundation 257
Antrobus, Dave 152
Apache 28, 29, 33, 211, 213, 272
Apache Joe 158
Apache Springs Ranch 236, 237
Apperson, Lou 125
Arias, Ignacio "Nacho" 232
Arivaca 28
Arivaca Ranch 168, 173
Arizona Historical Society 219
Arizona Republic 111
ASARCO 231
Ashcraft, John 23
Aycock, Beth Smith 207
Aycock, Bill 209

B

Babacomari creek 64
Babacomari Ranch 22, 190, 207, 211, 218
Babacomari Village 211
Baca Float 35
Backward B Spear Ranch 139
Baldwin, Emma 125
Bally Brophy 215
Barnes, Ray "Pete" 267
Barnett, Fred 170, 209
Bartlett, Chopeta 56, 57, 68
Bartlett, Fern 57, 68
Bartlett, Mark 55
Bartlett, Nellie 55, 57, 59, 60
Bartolo 158
Basinger, Pat 57
Basinger, Wayne 57
Bass, Arnold 107
Basurto, Mr. 181
Bellota Ranch 207
Bergier, Bob 39, 40
Bergier Ranch 254
Bergier, Ray 21, 28, 29, 35, 39, 42, 44
Bergier, Willie 39, 41, 44
Bermudez, Benjamin 221
Bettwy, Andrew 36
Bidegain, Pete 22, 212, 213
Bidegain, Todd 213
Blabon, Buck 20, 128
Black Oak Pioneer Cemetery 60, 83, 262, 263
Bland, Jess 81
Boice, Bob 176
Boice family 163
Boice, Frank 167
Boice, Gates & Johnson 168
Boice, Henry Gudgell 167, 168
Boice, Henry S. 167
Boice, Mary 169
Bond, Albert 25, 50
Bond Canyon 25
Bond, Catherine 25, 33
Bond, Charlotte 50
Bond, David 50

Wood, Henry 267
Wood, Mack 267
Woods, Herb 125
Woods, Jane 56, 60, 71, 169, 266
Woolley, Will 164
Wright, Clem 235
Wright, Wayne 235, 271
Wrightston, John 28, 35

X

XH Bar ranch 195

Y

Yakobian, George 256
Yaquis 105
Yeary, Jim 63
Yoas, Bird 41
Yoas, John 197
Yourgules, Frances 228
Yourgules, George 228
Yourgules, Isabel 228
Yourgules, Joe 228
Yourgules, Josefa 228, 229
Yourgules, Juan 228
Yourgules, Lena 228
Yourgules, Mike 229
Yourgules, Nikolas 228
Yourgules, Panchita 232

Z

Z Bar T Ranch 174
Z Triangle 237
Zary South Saddle Shop 176
Zula's Restaurant 224

Printed in the United States
60810LVS00004B/11-104